MARION DESCHAMPS was born i̇ tributed gastronomic and trav journals, including *Vogue, Hoι and Gardens, Ideal Home, Shι* others. She developed a taste fσ. .... cooking when she married a Frenchman and made her home in France over twenty years ago.

FRENCH
VEGETABLE COOKERY

MARION DESCHAMPS

ROBERT HALE · LONDON

© *Marion Deschamps 1978*

First published in Great Britain 1978
First paperback edition 1991

ISBN 0 7090 4353 8

Robert Hale Limited
Clerkenwell House
Clerkenwell Green
London EC1R 0HT

Printed in Great Britain by
St Edmundsbury Press Limited, Bury St Edmunds, Suffolk
and bound by Woolnough Bookbinders Limited

CONTENTS

For Jocelyne

INTRODUCTION

In France vegetables are most often served as a separate course and consequently the housewife pays particular attention to their preparation and serving. When they are merely an accompaniment to the meat, the meat often distracts from their poor cooking.

Their presentation falls naturally into five main categories: those served either with or after the meat course; more sustaining dishes which constitute a meal in themselves; soups; salads; and hors d'oeuvres.

The advantage of vegetables as an hors d'oeuvre is that they provide a light starter. For this either a single vegetable or a combination of them can be served with a French dressing or mayonnaise and often chopped onions. Particularly suitable for this treatment are leeks, French beans, peppers, beetroot, white haricot beans, broad beans, lentils, cauliflower and artichokes.

They can also be served in aspic and *à la grecque,* the latter, despite the name, being a very French method. They are popular, too, served as *crudités,* meaning uncooked. Tomatoes, grated carrots, grated celeriac, radishes and cucumber are good this way.

The pulses are particularly nutritious while all vegetables are valuable for their vitamins as well as adding eye-appeal to a dish.

The French, in fact, are true artists and their cooks know the importance of titillating the appetite with the attractive appearance of their food. Hors d'oeuvres and salads give full rein to their imagination. The continual serving of boiled potatoes and boiled cabbage is as tedious for the cook as for those for whom she prepares them.

Britain has always been fortunate in having a good supply of fresh vegetables, but now that so many of the exotic varieties are easily obtainable as well, the changes can be rung even more frequently.

When buying vegetables do not go for size since this is often obtained to the detriment of the flavour. It is also as well to remember that vegetables which are in season are always better, and of course less costly, than the forced varieties. *Primeurs*, as the French call the first spring vegetables, make this season a culinary enchantment with the delicious flavour of young carrots, new potatoes, tender peas and fresh salads.

Vegetables should not be stored longer than is absolutely necessary since they tend to lose their freshness and flavour. If circumstances, however, make storing necessary, green vegetables keep best in a covered container, thus preserving their moisture. Root vegetables should be peeled at once, plunged for two minutes into boiling water and drained before putting into the refrigerator. This method prevents oxidization.

Most green vegetables steam to perfection. The only justification for boiling them, a method which wastes most of their vitamins, is if the cooking water is used for soup.

Fresh vegetables should be put into fast-boiling water. Pulses, unless they are more than a year old, need no previous soaking. They should be put into cold water and, once boiling, any froth removed. Should it be necessary to add water during the cooking, this should be boiling.

The term *blanchissage* means putting certain vegetables, such as cabbage, celery and endives, for a few minutes into salted, boiling water. They are then rinsed quickly in cold water and left to drain. This is necessary before braising, a popular method of cooking vegetables, once steamed, with the addition of a little fat, onions and stock.

Gratiner means to brown in the oven with breadcrumbs or cheese and butter. *Au jus* means that, once the vegetables are cooked and drained, a knob of butter is added, together with a spoonful of flour and a little stock, and simmered for a further few minutes. Creamed and puréed are other good methods of serving vegetables. For this, once sieved, butter or cream are added. Vegetables which contain water such as French beans, cauliflower, sprouts and vegetable marrow should have a third of their volume of potato purée added.

Particular care should be paid to the washing of vegetables since if thoroughly clean it is often unnecessary to peel them.

Though I have used a sieve or vegetable mill in many recipes, a liquidizer can of course be used.

In the recipes given here quantities are sufficient for four.

Abbreviations

dsp	dessertspoon
tbsp	tablespoon
tsp	teaspoon
spf	spoonful

1

HERBS AND SPICES

Although most British kitchens have a good stock of dried herbs, spices and seasonings, and herb gardens have become popular during the past few years, there seems to remain a considerable lack of knowledge as to how to use them to best advantage.

A *bouquet garni,* or faggots of herbs, is frequently used in French cooking. It consists of sprigs of thyme, parsley and a bay leaf tied together and is cooked with the meat, fish or vegetable, always removed before serving. The term *fines herbes* usually includes parsley, tarragon, chives, chervil and watercress. It is particularly delicious in omelettes.

Parsley is the commonest of all herbs; fortunately, for it is rich in iron, calcium and vitamin C. Its medicinal value was greatly appreciated by the ancient Greeks and Romans.

Les simples, as the French call wild herbs, are 'simple' only in name. They have been known since the dawn of time, the Egyptians using them medically and even exporting them as far back as 4000 B.C. At about the same period a Chinese emperor wrote the first known work on the medicinal value of plants, citing a hundred herbs, both how to grow and to use them. Today considerable research is being made in order to ascertain how to benefit from them to the full.

The artistic value of parsley is also important, not just as a garnish but, chopped very fine, sprinkled over salads such as beetroot, tomatoes, potatoes, carrots and white haricot beans. When chopping herbs remember that it is easier to cut them with scissors in a cup than on a board, with the advantage that this way none of the precious juices are lost.

It should be remembered too, that the stalks contain as much flavour as the leaves.

When preparing, parsley should be plunged into boiling water before squeezing dry. A good way of taking a daily dose of vitamin C is to put a handful into a large glass of boiling water and leave it until cold.

Parsley can be kept for a considerable time if placed in a glass of water in a cool, dark place, changing the water daily. It can also be kept in a hermetically closed jar in the freezer.

Chervil, although seldom grown in Britain, is popular in France. A member of the parsley family, it is used in soups, salads and sauces.

Thyme is another very useful herb, a must for those with gardens or even a window-box. Not only is it essential in a *bouquet garni,* but is usually added to stews, to marinades and to fish when boiled. In France it often replaces tea as an infusion, being considered both a tranquillizer and good for the circulation.

Serpolet, sometimes referred to in French cooking, is, in fact, wild thyme.

Savory bears a certain resemblance to thyme but has a much more delicate flavour. It is used in *choucroutes,* with cucumber and with gherkins, and gives a particular lift to broad beans.

Bayleaves, the third essential to a *bouquet garni,* are also an excellent addition to many sauces. Crushed, they can be sprinkled, too, over grilled meat. They can be added to casseroles, to the skewers for kebabs and in the oil when frying potatoes. When dried, the leaves should be green, not brown.

Mint, used principally in Britain for mint sauce or added to peas and new potatoes, is seldom used in France except as an infusion, a custom introduced into the country from North Africa where mint tea is a common drink and considered a good stimulant. It is good, well chopped, with rice and potato salads. It has been known since antiquity, with mention of it in the Bible, while Greek physicians prescribed it as a cordial and tonic.

Sage, another favourite British herb, is also used in

France for stuffings. But it can be added, too, to the cooking water of green peas and haricot beans and gives a good flavour to baked fish.

Marjoram is also principally used for stuffings and for flavouring meat dishes. But it gives a lift, too, to carrots and turnips. While as an infusion, and sweetened with honey, it is considered good for insomnia.

Oregano is very similar in flavour.

The strong scent of rosemary means that it should be used sparingly. It is particularly to be recommended with pork and lamb and sprinkled over steak. A small sprig is also good in soups, fish, potato and egg dishes. As an infusion it is considered helpful for migraine.

Tarragon, best known in Britain for the excellence of tarragon wine vinegar, is another popular French herb. It is frequently used in sauces, particularly those which accompany fish and for stuffing chicken. It is also good, well chopped, sprinkled over salads, and it gives a lift to mayonnaise.

Another must for salads, particularly in the south of France, is basil which is also an essential to *pistou*, the vegetable soup of Provence. It is excellent, well chopped, in tomato and potato salads and also for flavouring stews and pasta. Like rosemary, it should be used sparingly, particularly in cooking when its flavour becomes even more pronounced. Like marjoram, as an infusion it is considered good for insomnia.

Numerous, in fact, are the herbs which give an extra zest to salads. You can ring the changes, as well, with parsley, chervil, mint, basil and chives; with the feathery leaves of fennel, bergamot leaves and sorrel, which is also used for soup, and with nasturtium flowers. While the berry-like seeds of nasturtium can be kept in vinegar and used, like capers, for sauces and flavouring. They are excellent in rice salads.

Other berries, those of the juniper, are used for spicing *choucroute,* for sauces, stuffings and in marinades. They are, incidentally, one of the chief flavourings of gin. The berries have important medical value, a dozen chewed daily being considered good for the digestion and for diabetics as well as for the pain of arthritis and toothache.

Spices, too, are great standbys for savoury cooking. Their very name evokes the mystery of undiscovered lands, for during the Middle Ages intrepid navigators took great risks to bring home the precious peppercorns and nutmeg, cinnamon and cloves among many others, while spice merchants became rich in their bartering.

From the sixteenth century onwards spices had a great influence on French cooking, although their extremely high prices put them as much in the luxury category as truffles are today.

Most used of all is the peppercorn. White pepper, hot and fiery, is that which is gathered when ripe, while the black variety is picked immature and has a more aromatic flavour. It is preferable to buy peppercorns and to grind them oneself, since once ground the aroma quickly deteriorates.

The very hot, pungent Cayenne pepper, red in colour, is obtained from capsicums. It is sold in powder form and should be used very sparingly.

Paprika, which is the name given by the Hungarians who use it widely in their cooking, is made from dried sweet peppers. It is good in many savoury dishes on account of its distinctive flavour and, since it is comparatively mild, it can be used generously.

Jamaican pepper, more commonly known as allspice, is the dried, unripe berry of the pimento tree. In French it is called *quatre épices* on account of its flavour which seems to be a blend of other spices. It is excellent for stuffings, soups, sauces and in all preparations of *charcuterie*.

Nutmeg is used frequently in French cooking, for pâtés and stuffings, pasta and with vegetables, particularly spinach. It is considered a stimulant, good for the circulation and for the digestion.

Cinnamon is nearly always added to apple dishes.

Cloves, too, are used with apples as well as in pâtés, stews and with red cabbage.

Ground cumin also goes well with red cabbage.

Coriander seeds, with their highly aromatic flavour, can be used in mixed vegetable dishes, with red cabbage, with game and in cold fish salad. They are sometimes used, too, in sauces that accompany meat as well as; once crushed, being scattered over steak.

Saffron, which comes from the crocus flowers, was introduced into France by the Arabs. It is an essential of *bouillabaisse* (the famous Provençal fish dish) as well as in other dishes of southern France. It is very expensive but a little goes a long way.

Mustard was popular with the ancient Romans whose soldiers introduced it into France. The brown variety has the most pungent flavour and for table use is often blended with the white seeds. In France it is sold, ready mixed, in jars and is mild in flavour. It includes a blend of herbs and spices mixed with vinegar. As well as an accompaniment to meat, sausages and bacon, it is good in salads and with mayonnaise. It stimulates the palate and aids the digestion, while externally it is used for poultices.

Lastly, salt, which is one of the earliest seasonings known to man, is an indispensable part of our diet. Rock or sea salt, in France called *gros sel,* is invaluable for cooking, while table salt, finer in texture, has the addition of sodium chlorate for free running.

There are other herbs and spices as well, but the ones mentioned here are those that are used in French cooking. Few cooks agree about quantities since it is a matter that can only be judged by one's own palate, thus giving plenty of scope in experimenting. Never, however, should herbs and spices be used indiscriminately.

2

ASPARAGUS

Asparagus, more than any other vegetable, is associated with spring since it is available from April to mid-June. Much appreciated by the ancient Romans, it was introduced into France during the reign of Louis XIV although in those days only the tips were eaten. A perennial of which there are 130 species, the three garden varieties are white, purple and green.

In France the plump white asparagus is favoured by gourmets, whereas the thinner green variety, although popular in Britain, is used on the Continent principally for soups and garniture on account of its more pronounced flavour. The purple kind, coming from Italy and the south of France, is the first to appear on the market.

Asparagus is a diuretic and the green tips contain vitamin C. It should always be eaten as fresh as possible, well washed and the spears peeled downwards with a sharp knife. The tough bottoms can be cut off and saved for soup.

The spears should then be tied together in bundles and boiled fast in salted water for about twenty minutes, or until they yield to a slight pressure with the finger. If the tips are very tender they can be covered with muslin to prevent breaking.

Once cooked, asparagus can be served either hot or cold. Served hot, the simplest method is with melted butter to which a little lemon juice should be added. For a more special occasion it can be served with a *hollandaise* sauce or its variations of a *maltaise* or *mousseline* sauce. When served cold, the most usual way is with a vinaigrette dressing or mayonnaise.

ASPERGES A LA VINAIGRETTE
(asparagus with French dressing)

Ingredients

2 lb asparagus	**¼ tsp mustard**
2 tbsp olive oil	**1 finely chopped shallot**
1 tsp vinegar	**seasoning**

Prepare and boil the asparagus. Drain well and cover with the well-mixed olive oil, vinegar, mustard, shallot and seasoning.

ASPERGES A LA MILANAISE

Ingredients

2 lb asparagus	**2 oz grated Parmesan**
2 oz butter	**cheese**

Once cooked, drain and arrange on a dish, the spears superposed so that all the tips are uncovered. Cover these tips with the Parmesan, dot with the butter and put under a hot grill until browned.

ASPERGES A LA POLONAISE

Ingredients

2 lb asparagus	**cupful finely chopped**
2 hardboiled eggs	**parsley**
2 oz butter	**2 tbsp fresh breadcrumbs**

Once cooked and drained, arrange the asparagus spears as in above recipe. Grate the eggs and mix with the parsley. Sprinkle this over the tips and cover with the melted butter mixed with the breadcrumbs.

ASPERGES A LA GENEVOISE
(asparagus with tartar sauce)

Ingredients

2 lb asparagus	seasoning
1 egg yolk	finely chopped shallot
juice of half a lemon	2 tsp chopped chives
½ tsp mustard powder	½ cup chopped parsley
olive oil as required	½ tsp chopped tarragon

Once cooked and drained, serve the asparagus with a tartar sauce made as follows. First make a mayonnaise by breaking the egg yolk into a basin with the mustard powder and beat. Then add the olive oil, drop by drop, beating all the time. When of creamy consistency add the lemon juice, then the shallot, chives, parsley, tarragon and seasoning.

ASPERGES A LA HOLLANDAISE

Ingredients

2 lb asparagus	2 oz butter
yolks of 3 eggs	juice of half a lemon
1 tbsp boiling water	½ tsp salt

Bring a pan of water to the boil and turn off the heat. In this stand a small pan containing the egg yolks and boiling water. Add a little of the butter, stir until it begins to thicken, then add more butter, continuing thus until all the butter is used and the sauce is of a creamy consistency. Add the salt and lemon juice. Great care should be taken not to allow the sauce to boil.

ASPERGES A LA MOUSSELINE

Ingredients

2 lb asparagus	2 oz butter
1 egg white	juice of half a lemon
yolks of 3 eggs	½ tsp salt
1 tbsp boiling water	2 oz cream

Proceed as for above recipe, adding, to the *hollandaise* sauce, the cream mixed with the well-whipped egg white.

ASPERGES A LA MALTAISE

Ingredients
2 lb asparagus
yolks of 3 eggs
1 tbsp boiling water

2 oz butter
juice of half a lemon
¼ tsp salt
1 orange

Proceed as for recipe *à la hollandaise* and to this sauce add the juice of the orange together with rind, previously grated and boiled for 5 minutes, and the eggs.

ASPERGES A LA CRÈME (1)

Ingredients
2 lb asparagus
1 tbsp olive oil
1 tbsp vinegar

½ tsp mustard powder
1½ tbsp cream
seasoning
¼ cup chopped chives

Cook and drain the asparagus. Mix together the olive oil, vinegar, mustard powder, cream, chives and seasoning. Serve this with the cold asparagus.

ASPERGES A LA CRÈME (2)

Ingredients
2 lb asparagus

2 oz cream
seasoning

Cook and drain the asparagus. Re-heat in pan, stirring in the cream and seasoning.

ASPERGES AU GRATIN
(baked asparagus)

Ingredients
2 lb asparagus
½ oz butter
1 oz flour
½ pint milk

a little grated nutmeg
2 tbsp grated Parmesan
  cheese
breadcrumbs

Cook and drain the asparagus. Put in an ovenproof dish and cover with a *béchamel* sauce made as follows. Melt the butter and stir in the flour. Add the milk, a little at a time and continue to stir until it thickens. Add seasoning, nutmeg and 1 tbsp of the cheese. Top with the remainder of the cheese mixed with the breadcrumbs and bake 10 minutes in a moderate oven.

ASPERGES POMPADOUR

Ingredients
2 lb asparagus
3 pints chicken broth

2 oz butter
yolks of 2 eggs
juice of half a lemon

Prepare the asparagus and boil in the chicken broth. Drain, preserving the broth. Melt the butter, stir in the egg yolks and the lemon juice and add half a pint of the broth. Cover the asparagus with this sauce.

OMELETTE AUX POINTES D'ASPERGE
(omelette with asparagus tips)

Ingredients
5 eggs
2 oz butter

few drops water
1 lb green asparagus
seasoning

Cut the tender part of the asparagus into small pieces and boil 10 minutes. Drain. Beat the eggs with the water and seasoning. Melt the butter and stir in the eggs. Lay the asparagus evenly over all the surface of the pan and finish cooking the omelette in the usual way.

ASPERGES AUX OEUFS BROUILLÉS
(scrambled eggs with asparagus tips)

Ingredients
1 lb green asparagus
5 eggs
3 oz butter

¼ pint milk
¼ pint cream
salt and pepper

Prepare the asparagus as in above recipe. Whisk the eggs with the salt and pepper. In a pan melt the butter and add the eggs, beating all the time. When they begin to thicken add the cream and asparagus. Serve immediately.

SOUFFLÉ D'ASPERGES

Ingredients	½ pint milk
1 lb asparagus	seasoning
1 oz butter	a little grated nutmeg
1 oz flour	4 eggs

Cook and drain the asparagus and crush with a fork. Make a *béchamel* sauce by melting the butter, stirring in the flour and gradually adding the milk. Continue to stir until it thickens. Add seasoning and nutmeg. Add the purée of asparagus and the beaten egg yolks. Allow to cool and then add the whites whisked until stiff. Put in a well-greased soufflé dish and bake 25 minutes, or until risen and golden.

ASPERGES EN COCOTTE
(asparagus in ramekins)

Ingredients	
½ lb green asparagus	8 dsp of cream
4 eggs	salt and pepper

Cut the asparagus into small pieces and boil 10 minutes. Drain. Well butter each ramekin and into each put a dsp of cream, the asparagus and seasoning. Cover with another spf of cream. Put the ramekins in a tin of water and bake 8 minutes in a moderate oven.

TARTE AUX ASPERGES

Ingredients	2 oz butter
1 lb green asparagus	1 oz flour
short pastry (2 oz butter	seasoning
to 5 oz flour)	2 oz grated Gruyère
2 hardboiled eggs	cheese

Prepare pastry and place in an 8-inch flan tin. Bake until firm but not golden. Cut the asparagus into small pieces and bake 10 minutes. Drain, preserving the cooking water. Cut the eggs into rounds and place on the tart. Make a sauce by melting the butter, stirring in the flour and adding, gradually, half a pint of the cooking water. Stir until it thickens. Cover the eggs with half of this sauce, then half of the asparagus, the remainder of the sauce and the remainder of the asparagus. Top with the grated cheese and bake 10 minutes, until golden.

3

BEANS

French, or green beans are one of the most delicious of summer vegetables. Preserved in Kilner jars, however, they lose little of their flavour. They also freeze well.

The best variety are those that are small, dark and stringless. All that is necessary is to top and tail them before washing in very hot water. Cold water tends to harden them. They should then be boiled in a minimum of salted water, uncovered, for fifteen minutes. Never overcook or they will become yellow if left too long in the water.

Should there be strings holding the two shells together, these should be removed. The larger runner beans should be sliced diagonally.

When very young and fresh they can simply be wiped and then steamed over a pan of boiling water with a tomato, onion and *bouquet garni*.

Although the traditional British method is to serve broad beans hot with a parsley sauce, there are other good ways of serving them such as a purée, in soups, or cold as an hors d'oeuvre. Except when very young, the skin should be removed. They are rich in calories.

Dried white haricot beans are particularly popular in France, served in various ways such as in a *cassoulet,* to accompany lamb and in salads. Like broad beans, they are rich in calories.

It is best to buy them when the past season's beans come into the shops in the late autumn. If really fresh, there is no need to soak them, but otherwise for between six to eight hours. If it is necessary to leave them for longer the water must be changed, or else they tend to ferment.

To cook, they should be put into tepid water and, once boiling, the water should be drained off. They should then be put into fresh water, together with an onion studded with two cloves, covered, and simmered until tender. Salt should never be added until the end of the cooking.

Kidney beans can be used in the same recipes as for haricots. Sometimes at the end of the cooking when the water has reduced, red wine and a little salt pork are added.

HARICOTS VERTS MAÎTRE D'HÔTEL

Ingredients   ½ cup chopped parsley
1 lb green beans   salt and pepper
1 oz butter   juice of half a lemon

Prepare the beans and boil in salted water for 15 minutes. Drain. Melt the butter, add the seasoning, parsley, lemon juice and beans and heat through.

HARICOTS VERTS AU BEURRE

Ingredients   2 oz butter
1 lb green beans   seasoning

Prepare the beans as in above recipe and drain. Melt the butter, add seasoning and re-heat the beans.

HARICOTS VERTS A LA CRÈME

Ingredients   salt and pepper
1 lb green beans   2 oz cream
1 oz butter   tsp chopped parsley

Prepare the beans as above and drain. Put the butter in a pan and stand this in a larger one of boiling water (the *bain-marie* method). When the butter has melted, stir in the cream, parsley and seasoning. Pour this sauce over the beans.

HARICOTS AU JUS

Ingredients
1 lb green beans

2 tbsp of the juices in
which a joint of meat
has been roasted

Prepare the beans as for above recipe. Drain and return to pan with the meat juices. Simmer 10 minutes.

HARICOTS VERTS A LA POULETTE

Ingredients
1 lb green beans
1 oz butter
1 oz flour

½ cup chopped parsley
1 finely chopped shallot
salt and pepper
1 egg

Prepare the beans as in above recipe. While they are draining, melt the butter, stir in the flour and then, gradually, a cupful of the water in which the beans were cooked. Add the seasoning, shallot, parsley and well-beaten egg. Cover the beans with this sauce.

HARICOTS VERTS EN SALADE (1)
(salad of green beans)

Ingredients
1 lb green beans
1 tsp chopped chives
1 tsp salt

pepper
2 tbsp olive oil
1 tbsp vinegar

Prepare and boil the beans. Drain well. When cold serve with a vinaigrette dressing made by mixing together the olive oil, vinegar, chives and seasoning.

HARICOTS VERTS EN SALADE (2)

Ingredients
1 lb green beans
seasoning
1 tsp vinegar

1 egg yolk
tsp mustard powder
olive oil as required

Prepare and boil the beans and drain. While still hot dress with a mayonnaise made as follows. Break the egg yolk into a bowl with the mustard powder and beat. Then add the olive oil, drop by drop, beating until of a creamy consistency. Add seasoning and vinegar. Serve very cold.

HARICOTS VERTS EN SOUFFLÉ

Ingredients

1 lb green beans	½ pint milk
2 oz butter	salt and pepper
1 oz flour	3 eggs
	2 oz cream

Prepare the beans and boil 20 minutes in salted water. Drain and sieve. Make a sauce by melting the butter, stirring in the flour and then, gradually, the milk. Blend until smooth. Allow to cool and fold in the egg yolks and the cream. Beat the egg whites until stiff and add. Put this mixture into a well-buttered soufflé dish and bake in a moderate oven for 25 minutes.

HARICOTS VERTS SAUTÉS

Ingredients

1 lb green beans	2 cloves garlic
pinch of grated nutmeg	seasoning
½ cup chopped parsley	2 oz grated Parmesan
2 oz olive oil	cheese

Prepare and boil the beans. Drain. Heat the olive oil and lightly fry the chopped garlic. Add the nutmeg, parsley, seasoning and beans and stir for a further few minutes. Sprinkle with the Parmesan cheese on serving.

HARICOTS VERTS A LA PROVENÇALE

Ingredients

1 lb green beans	3 ripe tomatoes
1 oz olive oil	1 clove garlic
1 large well-chopped onion	½ cup chopped parsley
	seasoning

Prepare the beans and boil 10 minutes in salted water. Drain and return to pan with the other ingredients. Simmer gently for 15 minutes.

FÈVES AU PERSIL
(broad beans with parsley sauce)

Ingredients
1 lb broad beans
2 oz butter

cupful chopped parsley
1 oz flour
seasoning

Shell the beans and boil 30 minutes in salted water. Drain. Make a sauce by melting the butter and stirring in the flour. Add, gradually, half a pint of the water in which the beans were boiled. Add parsley and seasoning and cover the beans with this sauce.

FÈVES A LA CROQUE AU SEL
(hors d'oeuvre of broad beans with salt)

Ingredients
1 lb very young broad
  beans

salt
bread and butter

Wash the beans, peel and serve, raw, dipped in salt accompanied by bread and butter.

FÈVES EN SALADE
(salad of broad beans)

Ingredients
1 lb broad beans
2 tsp finely-chopped onion

salt and pepper
2 tbsp olive oil
1 dsp vinegar

Shell the beans and boil 30 minutes. Drain. When still hot proceed as in the first recipe for salad of green beans.

FÈVES AU GRATIN
(baked broad beans)

Ingredients
1 lb broad beans
1 oz butter

1 oz cream
seasoning
cupful breadcrumbs

Prepare the beans and boil 30 minutes in salted water. Drain and sieve. Put in an ovenproof dish, mixing in the butter, cream and seasoning. Top with the breadcrumbs and bake 20 minutes in a moderate oven.

FÈVES MAÎTRE D'HÔTEL

Ingredients
1 lb broad beans
1 oz butter

½ cup chopped parsley
salt and pepper
juice of half a lemon

Prepare and cook the beans for 30 minutes. Then proceed as in the recipe for *haricots verts maître d'hôtel*.

HARICOTS ROUGES AU LARD
(kidney beans with bacon)

Ingredients
1 lb kidney beans
4 rashers of streaky
    bacon
2 shallots

2 oz butter
¼ pint red wine
1 tsp flour
seasoning

Prepare the beans and boil 20 minutes. Drain. Melt the butter and lightly fry the bacon rashers, chopped small, together with the sliced shallots. Add the flour, seasoning, wine and ¼ pint of the water in which the beans were cooked. Lastly, add the beans, cover and simmer 40 minutes.

HARICOTS BLANCS MAÎTRE D'HÔTEL

Ingredients
½ lb haricot beans
1 oz butter

½ cup chopped parsley
salt and pepper
2 shallots

Soak the beans if necessary. Then boil, together with shallots, until tender. Drain and proceed as in recipe for *haricots verts maître d'hôtel*.

HARICOTS BLANCS AU JUS

Ingredients
1 lb haricot beans
2 shallots

2 tbsp of the juices in
   which a joint of meat
   was roasted

Prepare and boil the beans. Drain and proceed as in recipe for *haricots verts au jus.*

HARICOTS BLANCS A LA CRÈME

Ingredients
½ lb haricot beans
1 onion
2 cloves

2 oz butter
1 oz flour
¼ pint cream
salt and pepper

Prepare the beans and boil until tender together with the onion stuck with the cloves. Melt the butter, stir in the flour and then, gradually, the milk. Blend well, add seasoning and cream. Add the drained beans and re-heat.

HARICOTS BLANCS EN SALADE
(salad of haricot beans)

Ingredients
½ lb haricot beans
2 shallots

salt and pepper
2 tbsp olive oil
1 tsp vinegar

Prepare the beans as above and drain. When cold, serve with a vinaigrette dressing made by mixing together the olive oil, vinegar, seasoning and well-chopped shallots.

HARICOTS BLANCS AU FOUR
(baked haricot beans)

Ingredients
½ lb haricot beans
1 large ripe tomato
2 garlic cloves
¼ lb mushrooms
2 tbsp chopped sage
salt and pepper

1 egg
cupful browned
   breadcrumbs
bouquet garni
½ cup dry white wine
1 oz olive oil

Prepare the beans and boil, together with the *bouquet garni* until tender. Remove *bouquet garni* and sieve haricots, stirring in the white wine. Add seasoning, sage, breadcrumbs and the well-beaten egg. Put into a well-greased ovenproof dish and bake 45 minutes in a moderate oven. Serve with a tomato sauce made by lightly frying the chopped garlic and mushrooms in the olive oil, then adding the crushed tomato and continuing to stir until well blended.

HARICOTS BLANCS EN PURÉE

Ingredients

¼ lb haricot beans	¼ pint milk or cream
2 oz butter	seasoning

Prepare and boil the beans until tender. Sieve. Add seasoning and return to pan. Over the fire work in the butter and cream.

HARICOTS BLANCS A LA BRETONNE

Ingredients

¼ lb haricot beans	1 very finely chopped onion
2 oz butter	¼ pint *coulis* of tomato
¼ pint milk or cream	(see page 188)
seasoning	1 tbsp chopped parsley

Prepare and boil the beans. Drain and return to pan with the *coulis,* onion, parsley and seasoning. Simmer 10 minutes, then stir in the cream and butter. Serve immediately.

HARICOT BLANCS EN BLANQUETTE
(stewed haricot beans)

Ingredients

¼ lb haricot beans	1 dsp flour
2 shallots	yolk of an egg
2 oz butter	¼ cup chopped parsley
	seasoning

Prepare and boil the haricots. Drain. Melt the butter and lightly fry the sliced shallots. Stir in the flour and ½ pint of the water in which the beans were boiled. Add beans and seasoning and simmer 10 minutes. Stir in the egg yolk and sprinkle with the parsley on serving.

4

THE CABBAGE FAMILY

Cabbage, Cauliflower and Brussels Sprouts

If cabbage, today, is probably the most despised of green vegetables, this is largely because it seems to suffer most from the British cook's lack of imagination in its preparation.

Yet in a past age it was held in high esteem and is probably the oldest known vegetable in the world. Pythagoras ranked it as one of the divine remedies. Hippocrates prescribed it, cooked in honey, as a remedy for diarrhoea and colic, while Cato claimed that it cured melancholy and induced good humour and that it accounted for the Romans' indomitable energy.

Hippocrates was not alone in lauding its medical value. The effects of heavy drinking were supposed to be prevented by eating it raw, previously macerated in vinegar. The Romans served it, boiled, at all their banquets.

In the last century a compress of cabbage macerated in borax was a popular cure for ulcers, while the leaves placed on the forehead were considered to relieve headaches.

Today we know it to be rich in iron, iodine, calcium and vitamins C, B_1 and K. The Germans recommend the juice of sauerkraut as a pick-me-up after injudicious eating and drinking. A French professor has made cabbage his base for a treatment of cirrhosis of the liver, although it is not recommended for those suffering from other liver complaints nor for goitre. Nor is it considered advisable for young children.

History shows that it was known in the far east since earliest times and that, with savoury stuffings, it was popular with the ancient Greeks. Sauerkraut, or *choucroute* as it is called in France, was in fact a Chinese invention. Cauliflower and broccoli, however, did not reach western Europe until the sixteenth century, and brussels sprouts not until the eighteenth.

Easily digestible, cabbage is nevertheless at its best in the form of *choucroute* which, although most usually served as *choucroute garnie* in which it is accompanied by sausages and ham, also makes an excellent soup and a good salad.

There are nearly a hundred different kinds of cabbage, the highest, up to 10 ft, being the tree or cow cabbage, cultivated in the Channel Islands for feeding cattle and whose stem is used to make walking sticks.

The three main varieties, however, are the common green cabbage, best used for soups and *potées,* the latter soups rich in meat and vegetables varying according to the region; the white cabbage and red cabbage.

When cooking red cabbage vinegar or lemon juice should be added to prevent its turning purple. Mixed with diced apples and spices it is an excellent accompaniment to pork and game. It is also good as an hors d'oeuvre and pickled.

White cabbages, too, make a good salad.

When buying, choose ones that are a good green colour and whose leaves are firm and tight. Where brussels sprouts are concerned, the small ones with tight leaves are far superior to those which look – and taste – more like a diminutive cabbage. With cauliflowers, look for a firm white head and bright-green leaves. Broccoli can usually be used in recipes given for cauliflower.

Brussels sprouts and cauliflower are included here as they belong to the cabbage family, and in France their name reflects the relationship, *choux de Bruxelles* being the name for brussels sprouts and *choufleur* for cauliflower.

The addition of a pinch of bicarbonate of soda during the cooking gives the cabbage a good colour, although it used to be supposed to destroy the vitamins. However, a new school of thought now claims this to be untrue since bicarbonate of soda preserves the greenness which is considered of nutritive value.

To make brussels sprouts more digestible they should be blanched in slightly salted water, then drained before being boiled or steamed. They have a better flavour when boiled in chicken broth.

The addition of a small muslin bagful of bread prevents the smell while cooking.

Green cabbage, kale and spring greens are best steamed as an accompaniment to the meat. They can then be served *au jus* which means that, once cooked, a little of the juices from a roast is added or else a knob of butter together with a spoonful of flour, and they are then simmered for a further few minutes. They are also good when braised.

To obtain the best flavour from the firm white cabbage it should be chopped small and then fried in an ounce of fat together with a sliced onion and a very little water.

CHOU EN SALADE
(cabbage salad)

Ingredients

1 small firm white cabbage	half a small red pepper
8 walnuts	2 tbsp olive oil
2 shallots	juice of half a lemon
8 black olives	seasoning

Thoroughly wash the cabbage and leave to drain. Chop the walnuts. Remove seeds from pepper and slice, together with the shallots. Shred the cabbage and mix well with the other ingredients.

CHOU BRAISÉ
(braised cabbage)

Ingredients

1 green cabbage	2 cloves
2 bacon rashers	*bouquet garni*
2 shallots	seasoning

Divide the cabbage into four, removing outer leaves and the hard core. Boil 5 minutes and drain. Put into a greased ovenproof dish together with the shallots, into which the cloves should be inserted, the *bouquet garni* and seasoning. Top with the bacon rashers, cover and bake very slowly for $1\frac{1}{2}$ hours.

CHOU AU FOUR
(cabbage hot-pot)

Ingredients

1 firm white cabbage	2 oz margarine
3 shallots	1 cup of stock
4 medium-sized potatoes	seasoning

Peel and parboil the potatoes. Slice the shallots and fry in the margarine until yellow. Grease an ovenproof dish and put in layers of cabbage, shallots and potatoes, finishing with potatoes. Add the stock, sprinkle with seasoning. Cover and cook in a moderate oven for half an hour. Remove lid and continue cooking until the potatoes are browned.

CHOU FARCI (1)
(stuffed cabbage)

Ingredients

1 large white cabbage	seasoning
1 large onion	1 large mushroom
clove of garlic	½ cup chopped parsley
1 cup of stock	1 cup breadcrumbs

Boil the cabbage for 15 minutes. Remove centre and chop this finely. Slice the onion and mushrooms and fry. Add to the chopped cabbage together with the other ingredients excepting the stock. Stuff the cabbage with this mixture, tie up with a string and put in a ovenproof dish. Add the stock and *bouquet garni* and bake 20 minutes in a moderate oven, basting frequently.

CHOU FARCI (2)

Ingredients

1 firm white cabbage	2 cloves garlic
bouquet garni	2 bacon rashers
1 lb chestnuts	1 oz Cognac
1 large onion	1 cup stock

Boil the cabbage fast for 5 minutes and drain. Boil the chestnuts and peel. Chop the onions and garlic and fry lightly with the chopped bacon rashers. Remove the centre of the cabbage and chop small. Mix with the sliced chestnuts, onions, garlic, bacon and seasoning. Add Cognac. Stuff cabbage with this mixture, tie up and put in an ovenproof dish. Add the stock and *bouquet garni.* Cover and bake 1 hour. Remove *bouquet garni* before serving.

CHOU AU GRATIN

Ingredients
1 firm white cabbage
1 large onion
2 oz butter
1 oz flour
½ pint milk
2 oz grated cheese
teacupful paprika, salt

Chop the cabbage and fry in 1 oz of the butter together with the sliced onion. Put in a greased ovenproof dish. Melt the remaining ounce of butter, stir in the flour and then, gradually, the milk. Stir till it thickens. Add cheese, salt and paprika. Cover cabbage with this sauce and sprinkle with breadcrumbs. Bake 10 minutes in a moderate oven.

FASSUM
(recipe from Provence)

Ingredients
1 small white cabbage
8 oz boiled rice
8 oz cooked peas
2 eggs
4 oz grated cheese
1 tbsp olive oil

Wash the cabbage and boil in salted water for 8 minutes. Remove the centre. Chop this well and mix with the rice, peas, cheese and well-beaten eggs. Season. Stuff cabbage with this mixture and put into an oiled ovenproof dish. Cook 20 minutes in a moderate oven.

CHOU ALSACIEN
(Alsatian-style cabbage)

Ingredients
1 small white cabbage
2 shallots
1 oz margarine
½ pint white wine
tcf finely chopped parsley

Shred the cabbage and fry in the margarine together with the shallots for 2 minutes. Add wine and simmer for 5 minutes, stirring at intervals. Add parsley on serving.

CHOU FERMIER
(farmhouse-style cabbage)

Ingredients	dsp cornflour
1 small white cabbage	2 oz cream
juice of a lemon	seasoning

Quarter the cabbage, removing the hard core, and steam for 45 minutes. Mix the cream and lemon juice with the cornflour, season and heat. Pour over the cabbage and serve immediately.

CHOU ROUGE EN SALADE (1)
(red cabbage salad)

Ingredients	2 bay leaves
4 cups shredded red cabbage	4 peppercorns
1 cup table salt	cupful vinegar
5 unpeeled garlic cloves	cupful red wine

Cover the cabbage with the salt and stand for 5 hours, stirring at intervals. Drain and put in a bowl with the garlic, bay leaves, peppercorns, vinegar and wine, previously boiled and left to cool. Marinate for 24 hours and drain well before serving.

CHOU ROUGE EN SALADE (2)

Ingredients	
4 cups shredded red cabbage	1 oz vinegar
	coriander seeds
½ pint red wine	seasoning

Boil the cabbage for 5 minutes in the wine and vinegar. Add the seasoning and coriander seeds and leave to cool. Pour off any surplus liquid before serving.

CHOU ROUGE A LA FLAMANDE
(sweet-sour red cabbage)

Ingredients	1 tsp vinegar
4 cups shredded red cabbage	cupful water
	1 dsp brown sugar
4 apples (preferably orange pippins) peeled, cored and quartered	2 cloves
	salt and pepper
	2 oz cooking fat

Put the cabbage in a pan together with the fat, vinegar, water and seasoning. Cover and simmer half an hour. Add the apples and sugar and continue cooking a further 10 minutes. Serve with roast pork.

CHOU ROUGE A LA LIMOUSINE
(red cabbage Limousin style)

Ingredients	1 lb chestnuts
4 cups shredded cabbage	2 oz fat
2 pints beef stock	seasoning

Peel the chestnuts and put in pan together with the cabbage, beef stock and seasoning. Bring to the boil and simmer 1 hour. Drain and stir in the fat. Return to heat for a further 2 minutes. Serve with pork or veal.

CHOU ROUGE BOURGUIGNON
(red cabbage Bourguignon style)

Ingredients	2 onions
4 cups shredded red cabbage	1 pint red wine
	seasoning
2 oz fat	2 oz flour

Fry the cabbage in the fat for 2 minutes together with the sliced onions. Add seasoning and the wine, bring to the boil and simmer 1 hour. Drain the cabbage and mix the flour with the wine in which it was cooked. Cover the cabbage with this sauce and serve with fried sausages.

CHOUFLEUR EN SALADE (1)
(cauliflower salad)

Ingredients

1 small cauliflower   4 oz olive oil
juice of a lemon   cupful finely chopped basil

Divide the cauliflower head into florets and put in a bowl with the oil and lemon juice. Stand for 2 hours, turning frequently. Put on to platter, season and garnish with the basil.

CHOUFLEUR EN SALADE (2)

Ingredients

1 small cauliflower   juice of half a lemon
cupful mayonnaise   2 finely chopped gherkins

Divide the cauliflower head into florets and boil for 8 minutes. Drain and mix with the mayonnaise while still hot. When cool, stir in the lemon juice, gherkins and seasoning.

CHOUFLEUR AU GRATIN
(cauliflower cheese)

Ingredients

1 cauliflower   3 oz grated cheese
3oz butter   breadcrumbs
1 oz flour   seasoning

Divide the cauliflower into quarters, removing the stem, and put into a pan of boiling water. Simmer 20 minutes. Drain, saving the water, and put the cauliflower into a well-greased ovenproof dish. Melt the butter, stir in the flour and add, gradually, half a pint of the water in which the cauliflower was cooked. Stir till it thickens, season and add 2 oz of the grated cheese. Pour this sauce over the cauliflower and cover with the remaining cheese mixed with the breadcrumbs. Bake 20 minutes in a moderate oven until the cheese is golden.

FRITOT DE CHOUFLEUR
(cauliflower fritters)

Ingredients

1 small cauliflower	juice of half a lemon
cupful finely chopped parsley	2 oz flour
	1 egg
seasoning	½ pint milk
3 oz olive oil	tomato sauce

Divide the cauliflower into florets and boil for 8 minutes. Drain well and put into a bowl with the olive oil and lemon juice. Leave for 2 hours, turning at intervals. Make a batter by putting the flour into a bowl and making a well in the centre. Into this break the egg and stir in the milk. Coat the cauliflower florets with the batter and fry in deep fat. Sprinkle with the parsley and accompany with the tomato sauce.

CHOUFLEUR EN COCOTTE

Ingredients

1 cauliflower	pint of stock
1 oz olive oil	8 new potatoes
1 oz butter	cooking fat from a roast
1 onion	seasoning

Divide the cauliflower into florets and plunge these into boiling water. Simmer 5 minutes. Drain. Put the oil and butter in a pan and fry the sliced onion until yellow. Add the cauliflower, potatoes, stock and seasoning. Simmer until tender, about 1 hour.

CHOUFLEUR MARINE

Ingredients

1 small cauliflower	2 cloves garlic
2 oz vinegar	small glassful white wine
2 cloves	*bouquet garni*
1 shallot	seasoning

Boil the onion, garlic, cloves and *bouquet garni* in the vinegar for 5 minutes. Divide the cauliflower into florets, having first removed the stem, and boil for 10 minutes. Drain. Put in pan with the vinegar mixture, add wine and seasoning and simmer a further 5 minutes. Stand 2 hours. Remove *bouquet garni*. Drain, add olive oil and serve, cold, as an hors d'oeuvre.

PAIN DE CHOUFLEUR
(cauliflower loaf)

Ingredients

1 small cauliflower	2 bacon rashers
2 oz breadcrumbs	2 eggs
seasoning	2 oz margarine
2 oz grated cheese	1 oz flour

Divide the cauliflower into the florets and boil until tender. Mash thoroughly and mix with the breadcrumbs, previously soaked in stock, the seasoning, and the bacon rashers previously fried and chopped small. Beat the eggs and add. Now make a white sauce by melting the margarine, stirring in the flour and then, gradually, half a pint of the water in which the cauliflower was boiled. Stir till it thickens. Put the cauliflower mixture into a well-greased ovenproof dish, cover with the sauce and top with the cheese. Bake three-quarters of an hour in a moderate oven.

CHOUX DE BRUXELLES AUX MARRONS
(brussels sprouts with chestnuts)

Ingredients

1 lb brussels sprouts	½ lb chestnuts
	2 oz butter

Make a purée of the chestnuts. Boil the sprouts, drain and add half the butter. Sieve, add to the chestnuts and add the remainder of the butter. Re-heat.

CHOUX DE BRUXELLES SAUTÉS

Ingredients

1 lb brussels sprouts	½ cup chopped parsley
2 oz butter	seasoning

Either steam or boil the sprouts. Once cooked, drain well. Melt the butter, add seasoning and fry the sprouts for 3 or 4 minutes, turning all the time. Serve sprinkled with the parsley.

CHOUX DE BRUXELLES FERMIÈRE
(brussels sprouts farmhouse style)

Ingredients

1 lb brussels sprouts

chicken broth

1 oz butter

4 bacon rashers

seasoning

Boil the sprouts in the broth until tender. Drain. Lightly fry the chopped bacon rashers, then put with the sprouts and seasoning in an ovenproof dish. Dot with the butter and bake 15 minutes.

CHOUX DE BRUXELLES A LA CRÈME

Ingredients

1 lb brussels sprouts

4 oz butter

2 oz cream

seasoning

Put the sprouts in a pan and cover with water. When half cooked, drain and finish cooking in the butter. Stir in the cream and serve immediately.

PURÉE DE CHOUX DE BRUXELLES A LA FLAMANDE
(Flemish-style purée of brussels sprouts)

Ingredients

1 lb brussels sprouts

2 oz butter

$\frac{1}{4}$ lb potatoes

2 bacon rashers

Boil or steam the sprouts. Drain and pass through vegetable mill. Peel and boil the potatoes until tender and sieve. Add to the sprouts together with the bacon, previously fried and chopped small, and the seasoning. Re-heat.

5

CARROTS

The carrot is one of the cook's most valuable vegetables, an essential for flavouring stews, soups and stock.

It is known to have been cultivated in Europe from early times and in Britain at least since the sixteenth century. In the reign of Charles II it was the fashion for ladies to wear carrot leaves instead of feathers in their hats.

They are at their best between May and October. For those with gardens they keep well if dug up in October, the leaves cut off, and put into sand.

Rich in vitamins and in mineral salts, they stimulate growth in young children while a carrot broth is particularly recommended for infantile diarrhoea.

There are a number of varieties but it is only the red (or orange) carrot that is used for human consumption. When buying, choose, for preference, those that are a deep colour and crisp. Whenever possible, it is best to scrape rather than peel them. For older ones, the woody core should be removed since it is this which gives a bitter flavour.

Ways of serving them are numerous and they are particularly nutritive when eaten raw, either grated as an hors d'oeuvre or scattered over a green salad. To accompany a roast they are good when served, as the French call it, *au jus*, meaning that, once cooked and drained, they are re-heated with a little of the fat in which the meat was roasted.

CAROTTES RAPÉES (1)
(grated carrots)

Ingredients

¼ lb young carrots
2 tbsp olive oil
juice of half a lemon
seasoning
¼ cup chopped parsley

Well scrub and grate the carrots. Dress with the well-mixed oil, lemon juice and seasoning, and garnish with the chopped parsley.

CAROTTES RAPÉES (2)

Ingredients

¼ lb young carrots
1 tsp vinegar
1 egg yolk
seasoning
tsp mustard powder
olive oil as required

Well scrub and grate the carrots and mix with a mayonnaise made as follows: break the egg yolk into a bowl with the mustard powder and beat; add the olive oil, drop by drop, beating all the time; when of a creamy consistency add the vinegar and seasoning.

SALADE BRETONNE

Ingredients

3 large carrots
2 medium-sized onions
2 medium-sized tomatoes
salt
tsp Cayenne pepper

Boil the carrots, drain and pass through vegetable mill. Lightly fry the sliced onions and tomatoes in olive oil and mix with the carrots. Add salt and Cayenne pepper and serve very cold.

CAROTTES A LA CRÈME

Ingredients

1 lb carrots
1 dsp sugar
1 tsp salt
¼ pint cream

For small carrots leave whole. For larger ones, cut in rounds. Put in a pan together with the salt and sugar, cover with water. Bring to the boil and simmer 45 minutes or until they have absorbed nearly all the water. Stir in the cream and heat through.

CAROTTES AU BEURRE

Ingredients
1 lb young carrots
1 oz butter

½ cup chopped parsley
tsp lemon juice
seasoning

Prepare the carrots and boil until tender. Drain. To the carrots add the butter, parsley, lemon juice and seasoning. Simmer a further 2 minutes, stirring well.

CAROTTES A LA BÉCHAMEL
(carrots in white sauce)

Ingredients
1 lb carrots
½ oz butter
2 tbsp flour

½ pint milk
yolk of an egg
pinch of grated nutmeg
seasoning

Prepare the carrots and boil until tender. Drain and mix well with a *béchamel* sauce made by melting the butter, stirring in the flour and adding, gradually, the milk. Stir until it thickens and add the nutmeg and seasoning.

CAROTTES A LA MAÎTRE D'HÔTEL

Ingredients
1 lb young carrots
½ teacup chopped parsley

stock
2 oz butter

Prepare the carrots and boil for 30 minutes in the stock. Drain. Melt the butter and add the carrots, parsley and seasoning. Fry for a few minutes and serve immediately.

CAROTTES AU GRATIN
(baked carrots)

Ingredients

1 lb young carrots	1 dsp paprika
2 oz margarine	salt
2 oz flour	breadcrumbs
¼ pint milk	4 oz grated cheese

Prepare the carrots and boil until tender. Drain. Melt the margarine, stir in the flour and then, gradually, the milk. Stir until it thickens. Add the salt, paprika and half of the grated cheese. Mix with the carrots and put in a well-greased ovenproof dish. Top with the remainder of the cheese mixed with the breadcrumbs. Bake 20 minutes in a moderate oven.

CAROTTES GLACÉES
(glazed carrots)

Ingredients

1 lb carrots	1 oz sugar
1 oz salt	3 oz butter

Prepare the carrots and cut in rounds. Young ones should be brought to the boil and drained, old ones boiled for 8 minutes before draining. Return to pan with the salt, sugar and butter. Cover with water and simmer until the water is almost entirely absorbed and has the consistency of syrup.

CAROTTES AUX FINES HERBES
(carrots with herbs)

Ingredients

1 lb young carrots	¼ cup chopped parsley
1 breakfastcup water	¼ cup chopped chervil
2 oz butter	tbsp chopped chives
½ oz sugar	seasoning

Prepare the carrots, cut lengthwise, and simmer in the water, sugar and butter until tender and the liquid is almost absorbed. Add the herbs and seasoning and continue cooking a further 5 minutes.

CAROTTES A LA POULETTE

Ingredients	*bouquet garni*
1 lb young carrots	yolks of 2 eggs
2 oz butter	tsp of sugar
1 tbsp cornflour	seasoning

Parboil the carrots with the *bouquet garni* and drain, reserving a little of the cooking water. Melt the butter, stir in the flour and two tablespoons of the cooking water. Add the carrots, sugar and seasoning and continue cooking gently for 5 minutes. Whisk the egg yolks with a little melted butter and add. Serve immediately.

CAROTTES A LA BOURGUIGNONNE
(carrots Burgundian style)

Ingredients	
1 lb carrots	cupful stock
2 oz butter	2 oz flour
2 onions	seasoning

Prepare and chop the carrots and boil until tender. Drain. In a pan melt 1 oz of the butter and lightly fry the sliced onions until yellow. Stir in 1 oz of the flour and the stock. When smooth, add the carrots and seasoning. Cover and simmer 10 minutes. Serve with a mustard sauce made by melting the remaining 2 oz of butter, stirring in the remaining ounce of flour together with the mustard. Add a cupful of the liquid in which the carrots were boiled and stir until the consistency of a white sauce.

CAROTTES VICHY
(carrots Vichy style)

Ingredients	
9 large carrots	juice of 2 lemons
½ oz butter	seasoning

Cut carrots in very thin strips and put in a large flat pan with the butter and seasoning. Add sufficient water to come level with the bottom layer. Cover and bake in a slow oven. When half cooked add the lemon juice and continue cooking until tender.

CAROTTES SAUTÉES
(fried carrots)

Ingredients	4 cloves garlic
1 lb carrots	3 bacon rashers
2 oz margarine	seasoning

Parboil the carrots and drain. Slice. Melt the margarine and fry the carrots together with the chopped bacon, garlic and seasoning until the carrots are browned.

PAIN DE CAROTTES
(carrot loaf)

Ingredients	½ pint milk
1 lb carrots	seasoning
2 eggs	¼ lb mushrooms
2 oz margarine	1 large tomato
1 oz flour	2 cloves garlic

Prepare the carrots and boil until tender. Pass through vegetable mill. Make a white sauce with 1 oz of the margarine, the flour and the milk. Season and add to the carrots. Add the well-beaten eggs. Put into a well-greased ovenproof dish. Put this into a larger dish, half filled with water (the *bain-marie* method) and bake 40 minutes in a moderate oven. Serve with a tomato sauce made by melting the remaining ounce of margarine and lightly frying the sliced mushrooms and garlic. Add the sliced tomato and simmer a further 2 minutes.

CAROTTES FERMIER
(farmhouse-style carrots)

Ingredients	seasoning
¼ lb carrots	½ pint milk
1 tbsp sugar	1 tbsp flour
2 oz butter	cupful yoghourt

Prepare the carrots, cut into rounds and simmer in the milk together with the sugar and seasoning until tender. Drain, reserving the liquid. Melt the butter, stir in the flour and the milk in which the carrots were boiled. Stir till it thickens. Add the yoghourt and return carrots to this sauce. Heat through.

CAROTTES A LA SÉVILLE
(Seville-style carrots)

Ingredients	2 oz butter
1 lb carrots	tsp sugar
cupful pre-soaked raisins	seasoning

Prepare the carrots and cut into rounds. Melt the butter in a heavy pan and put in the carrots together with the sugar and seasoning. Add $\frac{1}{4}$ pint of water, cover hermetically and simmer gently for 1 hour, stirring at intervals. Add the raisins, mixing well, and simmer a further 20 minutes.

CAROTTES A L'ANDALOUSE
(Andalusia-style carrots)

Ingredients	1 egg
1 lb carrots	1 tbsp brandy or cognac
1 oz flour	pinch of grated nutmeg
$\frac{1}{2}$ oz butter	seasoning

Cook the carrots until tender. Drain and pass through vegetable mill. Stir in the butter, flour, cognac, seasoning, nutmeg and the yolk of the egg. Whisk well the white and add. Form into balls, flattening top and bottom, and fry until golden.

6

GOURDS

The name of 'gourd' usually evokes the ornamental variety. Yet vegetable marrows, courgettes, pumpkins, cucumbers and gherkins are all part of this family, to be found in Asia, northern America and Europe. They have little nutritive value.

In France the delicate small *courgette* is more popular than the large marrow, or *courge*. While pumpkins, which can weigh up to 110 lb are used principally for soup although in country districts they are prepared in other ways as well.

Cucumbers, in Britain, appear invariably in sandwiches or a mixed salad. Yet carefully prepared they make a good salad on their own. There are also various ways of serving them hot. As the season advances and they tend to become watery the seeds should be removed. They are used, too, in beauty preparations on account of the softening effect on the skin. For those who find them indigestible they should be covered in salt and left for twelve hours. This draws off the juice which is the only indigestible part.

Gherkins are very popular in France, whether in a rice salad, with cold meat or a *pot-au-feu*, and they are nearly always served with *charcuterie*. They are easy to cultivate and simple to bottle.

COURGE AU GRATIN
(vegetable marrow in the oven)

Ingredients	
1 small vegetable marrow	2 oz grated cheese
2 oz breadcrumbs	1 oz butter
	1 oz flour

Peel the marrow and remove seeds. Dice and boil for 10 minutes, or until tender. Drain, reserving the liquid. Melt the butter, stir in the flour and then, gradually, half a pint of the water in which the marrow was boiled. Stir till it thickens. Put the marrow in an ovenproof dish, cover with the sauce and top with the cheese mixed with the breadcrumbs.

COURGE AU FROMAGE BLANC
(vegetable marrow stuffed with cream cheese)

Ingredients

4 slices of vegetable marrow about 4 ins in length and 2 ins wide	clove of garlic
	1 shallot
	seasoning
2 eggs	cupful browned
herbs as available	breadcrumbs

Boil the pieces of marrow until tender but still firm. Scoop out the interior and mix with the cream cheese, well-beaten eggs, finely chopped garlic and shallot, herbs and seasoning. Return to the marrow shells, arrange in an ovenproof dish and top with the breadcrumbs. Bake 20 minutes in a moderate oven.

SOUFFLÉ A LA COURGE

Ingredients

half a medium-sized vegetable marrow	1 oz butter
	1 oz flour
3 eggs	½ pint milk
2 oz grated cheese	salt and pepper

Peel the marrow, remove seeds, dice and boil until tender. Sieve. Melt the butter, stir in the flour and then, gradually, the milk. Stir until it thickens. Cool and add the egg yolks and seasoning. Whip the egg whites until stiff and fold into the marrow mixture. Put this into a well-buttered soufflé dish. Top with the grated cheese and bake 25 minutes in a hot oven, or until well risen.

BEIGNETS A LA COURGE
(vegetable marrow fritters)

Ingredients

half a medium-sized vegetable marrow	2 oz flour
1 lemon	¼ pint milk
1 egg	¼ pint water
	seasoning

First prepare the batter by putting the flour and seasoning into a bowl and making a well in the centre. Break the egg into this and beat well. Add milk gradually. Cover with a cloth and leave in a warm place for 2 hours. Peel and remove seeds from the marrow, cut into finger lengths and boil until tender but still firm. Drain. Dip the marrow pieces in the batter mixture and fry in deep fat. Serve with the lemon juice.

COURGE SAUTÉE
(fried marrow)

Ingredients

half a vegetable marrow	2 bacon rashers
2 oz olive oil	salt and pepper
3 cloves garlic	juice of half a lemon

Peel the marrow and cut very thin as for potato chips. Fry, together with the chopped garlic and bacon, in the olive oil until crisp and golden. Sprinkle with the seasoning and lemon juice.

COURGETTES AU BEURRE

Ingredients

4 baby marrows	2 tbsp chopped chives
2 oz butter	juice of a lemon
2 tbsp finely chopped parsley	seasoning

Slice the unpeeled baby marrows and boil in a minimum of water for 10 minutes. Drain well. Return to pan with the parsley, chives, butter and seasoning. Simmer 2 minutes, turning frequently, and serve sprinkled with the lemon juice.

COURGETTES A LA GRECQUE

Ingredients

4 baby marrows	bouquet of thyme, bay
1 oz olive oil	leaf and celery tied
½ pint water	together
½ pint dry white wine	1 oz olive oil
½ tsp coriander seeds	seasoning
4 small onions	½ cup chopped parsley

Slice the unpeeled baby marrows and put in a pan with the wine, water, bouquet, coriander seeds and seasoning. Bring to the boil and simmer 10 minutes. Leave to cool in the liquid. Drain, removing bouquet, add the olive oil and serve very cold sprinkled with the parsley.

COURGETTES EN SALADE
(salad of baby marrows)

Ingredients

4 baby marrows	2 tbsp olive oil
1 tbsp each of chopped	1 tbsp vinegar
parsley, chervil and	1 finely chopped onion
tarragon	salt and pepper

Cut the unpeeled baby marrows into slices and boil for 8 minutes. Drain well. When cold mix with the olive oil, vinegar, onion, seasoning and herbs.

TIAN DE COURGETTES
(baby marrows as prepared in Provence)

Ingredients

4 baby marrows	2 oz rice
a little grated nutmeg	2 oz grated cheese
1 clove garlic	½ cup chopped parsley
2 oz olive oil	3 slices stale bread

Prepare and slice the baby marrows and fry gently in the olive oil, together with the nutmeg, seasoning and chopped garlic clove until tender. Add the previously boiled rice and continue cooking 5 minutes, stirring frequently. Add 1 oz of the grated cheese and put this mixture into an earthenware vegetable or gratin dish; a *tian* is the name of the dish used in Provence from which this recipe takes its name. Cover with the bread slices previously dipped in water and squeezed out. Sprinkle with the remaining grated cheese and bake in a moderate oven until golden.

FONDUE DE COURGETTES

Ingredients

4 baby marrows	1 oz grated cheese
2 hardboiled eggs	¾ pint milk
cupful of fresh	2 oz butter
breadcrumbs	1 oz flour
1 oz olive oil	seasoning

Cut the baby marrows into finger lengths and fry in the olive oil until tender, then put in an ovenproof dish. Soak the breadcrumbs in a ¼ pint of the milk. Make a sauce by melting the butter, stirring in the flour and then, gradually, the remaining ½ pint of milk. Season and stir until it thickens. In a bowl crush the hardboiled eggs and add the squeezed-out bread, the cheese and the sauce. Mix well together. Cover the fried marrow with this mixture and bake 20 minutes in a moderate oven.

POTIRON EN PURÉE

Ingredients	salt and pepper
½ lb pumpkin	yolks of 2 eggs
1 oz butter	1 oz cream

Peel the pumpkin, removing seeds. Dice and boil in salted water until tender. Sieve. Lightly fry the sliced onion in the butter, add the sieved pumpkin and the seasoning and simmer 10 minutes. Add the well-beaten egg yolks and the cream on serving.

POTIRON AU GRATIN
(baked pumpkin)

Ingredients

¼ lb pumpkin	2 oz grated cheese
2 oz butter	seasoning
1 oz flour	2 eggs
¼ pint milk	pinch of nutmeg

Prepare and sieve the pumpkin as in the above recipe. Make a sauce by melting 1 oz of the butter, stirring in the flour and then, gradually, the milk. Stir until it thickens. Add this to the pumpkin purée together with the seasoning, well-beaten eggs, nutmeg and cheese. Put this mixture into a ·well-greased ovenproof dish. Top with the remaining butter and bake 20 minutes in a moderate oven.

POTIRON A L'AMÉRICAINE
(roast pumpkin)

Ingredients

1 lb pumpkin cut into slices	tsp each of powdered cinnamon, ground ginger and powdered sage
salt and pepper	
2 oz butter	

Peel the pumpkin, removing seeds and arrange the slices on a well-greased baking tin. Sprinkle with the cinnamon, ginger, sage and seasoning. Top with the butter and bake in a moderate oven until tender, basting frequently.

POTIRON A L'ARDENNAISE

Ingredients

¼ lb of pumpkin	seasoning
4 onions	3 slices stale bread

Peel the pumpkin, remove seeds and dice. Boil until tender in salted water and drain. Fry the sliced onions and put a layer of these at the bottom of an ovenproof dish. Add the pumpkin and then the remaining onions. Bake 20 minutes in a moderate oven. On serving top with *croûtons* (the stale bread cut into cubes and fried in butter).

SALADE DE CONCOMBRE
(cucumber salad)

Ingredients

1 small cucumber	**pepper**
cupful finely chopped	**juice of half a lemon**
parsley	**tsp vinegar**

Peel the cucumber very thinly, put in a colander and cover with a thin layer of kitchen salt. Leave for 5 minutes. Turn and leave for another 5 minutes. Wash in several lots of water, drain and dress with the pepper, parsley, lemon juice and vinegar. It is a matter of taste whether or not olive oil is added.

CONCOMBRE A LA CRÈME (1)

Ingredients

1 small cucumber	**3 tbsp cream**
juice of half a lemon	**seasoning**

Prepare as in above recipe. Once drained, dress with the cream, lemon juice and seasoning.

CONCOMBRE A LA CRÈME (2)

Ingredients

1 small cucumber	**1 tbsp flour**
2 oz butter	**¼ pint milk**
2 tbsp cream	**1 dsp paprika**
	salt

Peel the cucumber and chop fairly thickly. Boil fast for 2 minutes and drain. Return to pan with 1 oz of the butter for a further 2 minutes. Make a sauce by melting the remaining ounce of butter, stirring in the flour and then, gradually, the milk. Add the salt, paprika and cream, and blend well.

CONCOMBRE AU BEURRE

Ingredients
1 small cucumber
1 tsp vinegar

2 oz butter
juice of a lemon
cupful chopped parsley

Peel the cucumber, slice and cover with water to which salt and the vinegar has been added. Boil 8 minutes and drain. Return to pan with the butter, parsley and lemon juice and turn until heated through.

CONCOMBRE A LA BORDELAISE

Ingredients
1 small cucumber
1 oz olive oil
1 oz butter

flour
¼ pint red wine
salt and pepper
2 cloves

Peel the cucumber, cover with a thin layer of salt and leave 5 minutes. Turn and leave another 5 minutes. Rinse and drain well. Dip in the flour and dry in the oil and butter. Add the wine, pepper and cloves and simmer gently for 20 minutes.

CONCOMBRE MAÎTRE D'HÔTEL

Ingredients
1 small cucumber
1 oz butter

½ cup chopped parsley
salt and pepper
juice of a lemon

Peel and slice the cucumber. Boil 5 minutes and drain well. Melt the butter, add the seasoning, lemon juice and cucumber, and heat through.

CONCOMBRE A LA POULETTE

Ingredients
1 small cucumber
1 oz butter
1 oz flour

½ cup finely chopped parsley
1 finely chopped shallot
salt and pepper
1 egg

Prepare the cucumber as in above recipe. While draining, melt the butter, stir in the flour and then, gradually, a cupful of the water in which the cucumber was boiled. Add seasoning, shallot, parsley and well-beaten egg. Cover cucumber with this sauce.

CONCOMBRE FARCIE
(stuffed cucumber)

Ingredients

1 medium-sized cucumber	**1 tbsp chopped mint**
1 cup rice	**seasoning**

Boil and drain the rice. When cold, mix with the mint and seasoning. Peel the cucumber and cut into thick pieces about 2 inches in length. Scoop out the centres and fill cavities with the rice mixture.

CORNICHONS AU VINAIGRE
(preserve of gherkins in vinegar)

Cover some gherkins with kitchen salt and leave for 24 hours. Drain and wipe well. Put in jars with a few small onions and fill up with vinegar. Cover.

CORNICHONS AU GROS SEL
(preserve of gherkins in kitchen salt)

Wipe 1 lb gherkins and put in an earthenware receptacle. Spread over them 2 cups kitchen salt and pepper. Cover with 2 parts water to 1 part vinegar and a few sprigs of tarragon. Leave in a warm place for a week, when they are ready for consumption. Prepared this way they keep for only a few weeks and should be put, for preference, in the refrigerator.

7

LUXURY VEGETABLES

Artichokes, Aubergines, Fennel, Peppers and Avocado Pear

If the vegetables given here are considered a luxury, it is simply because, being imported, they are more expensive than those that are home grown.

The most popular of these in France, where it is relatively cheap, is the globe artichoke.

Its unique slightly nutty flavour makes it the most delicate of green vegetables. Old records show that it was cultivated in ancient Rome, in Greece, Egypt and Asia. It is rich in vitamin C.

Those on the British market come chiefly from Brittany. When shopping, choose ones that are a bright green colour and have tightly packed leaves.

A kind of thistle, there are three main parts. Once cooked, the outer leaves should be pulled off separately with the fingers, the succulent ends dipped into the sauce of your choice and prized off with the teeth. The choke, which is the fuzzy core, is cut out. The heart, or bottom of the lower section and eaten with knife and fork, is the most delectable part.

They should be boiled in salted water for between thirty-five and forty minutes and are cooked when an outer leaf can be detached with the fingers.

The aubergine, or eggplant, evokes the more exotic dishes of warmer countries. It originated in India and is to be found all along the Mediterranean, a reason why olive oil is used in nearly all its preparations.

It is usually cooked unpeeled, the skin being responsible for much of its fine flavour. It should first be sprinkled with salt to extract the excessive water and somewhat bitter juices. Most of the recipes improve with re-heating.

Fennel, with its pronounced aniseed flavour, is also cultivated principally in Mediterranean countries.

The feathery leaves can be used for flavouring sauces. So, too, can the stalks which are often dried. This is probably why it is sometimes referred to as a herb. Fennel sauce is particularly popular with fish. The bulbous stem is usually boiled, while the leafy stalk can be cut off and eaten raw as a salad with a vinaigrette dressing. It is considered good for constipation.

Sweet peppers, or *poivrons,* are sometimes confused with the small red and very hot chillies from which Cayenne pepper is made. They are good raw, sprinkled over salads, in which case red ones should be used since, being ripe, they are more digestible.

The avocado pear is prevalent in South America and the West Indies although those on the European markets come mostly from Israel.

Served as an hors d'oeuvre, half a pear per person is sufficient since the buttery consistency of the pulp is very sustaining. They are cheapest between May and September.

Once cut, sprinkling them with lemon juice helps to prevent discoloration. Should this occur, however, one has only to scrape off the upper layer or simply mash it well in.

ARTICHAUTS A LA VINAIGRETTE
(globe artichokes with French dressing)

Ingredients

4 globe artichokes	1 dsp vinegar
4 tbsp olive oil	salt and pepper

Wash the artichokes very thoroughly and boil in salted water until tender (about 30 minutes). Drain upside down and serve, cold, with a French dressing made by mixing together the olive oil, vinegar and seasoning.

ARTICHAUTS A LA GRECQUE

Ingredients

8 globe artichokes	juice of a lemon
2 oz olive oil	seasoning
bouquet garni	1 tsp coriander seeds
	½ pint dry white wine

With a sharp knife cut off the leaves close to the stem. Scoop out the chokes from the centres and remove the hearts. Put these in a pan together with the other ingredients. Add a little water if necessary to cover, bring to the boil and simmer 20 minutes. Leave to cool in this liquid.

ARTICHAUTS A LA HOLLANDAISE

Ingredients

4 globe artichokes	2 oz butter
yolks of 3 eggs	juice of half a lemon
1 tbsp boiling water	½ tsp salt

Thoroughly wash the artichokes and cook in boiling, salted water until tender. Drain upside down and serve, hot, with a *hollandaise* sauce made as follows. Bring a pan of water to the boil and turn off the heat. In this stand a small pan containing the egg yolks and water. Add a little of the butter, stir until it begins to thicken, then add more butter, continuing thus until all the butter is used and the sauce has a creamy consistency. Add the salt and lemon juice. Great care should be taken not to allow the sauce to boil.

FONDS D'ARTICHAUTS SAUTÉS

(fried artichoke hearts)

Ingredients

8 globe artichokes	2 oz butter
1 oz flour	1 oz olive oil

Slice the artichoke hearts, sprinkle with the lemon juice and seasoning and stand for an hour. Heat the oil and butter and fry the hearts in this for 4 minutes on each side.

ARTICHAUTS A LA BARIGOULE

Ingredients

4 globe artichokes	4 bacon rashers
4 oz chopped ham	salt and pepper
1 oz chopped parsley	¼ pint white wine
¼ lb mushrooms	3 oz olive oil

Cut off the stems of the artichokes close to the base and remove chokes. Fry gently in 2 oz of the olive oil for 10 minutes. Then fill centres with the ham, parsley, finely chopped mushrooms and the remaining ounce of olive oil. Wrap a bacon rasher round each and return to pan. Add wine, cover, and simmer for 1 hour.

ARTICHAUTS FARCIS
(stuffed globe artichokes)

Ingredients

4 globe artichokes	¼ cup chopped parsley
1 cup white breadcrumbs	1 onion
¼ pint milk	3 oz button mushrooms
	4 bacon rashers

Thoroughly wash the artichokes, remove stems and boil fast in salted water for 30 minutes. Drain well and remove chokes. Replace these by a stuffing made as follows. Soak the breadcrumbs in the milk and squeeze out. Mix this with the chopped bacon, onion and mushrooms all previously fried. Add the parsley and butter. Put the stuffed artichokes in an ovenproof dish, having first covered the bottom with olive oil. Bake 20 minutes in a moderate oven.

ARTICHAUTS A L'ITALIENNE

Ingredients

8 artichoke hearts	2 oz grated Parmesan
juice of half a lemon	cheese
¼ pint white wine	½ cup breadcrumbs
2 oz butter	seasoning

Boil the artichoke hearts for 10 minutes and drain. Melt 1 oz of the butter, stir in the flour and then, gradually, the wine. Add lemon juice and seasoning and stir till it thickens. Put hearts in a buttered ovenproof dish, pour the sauce over them and top with the grated cheese and breadcrumbs mixed together. Dot with the remaining butter and brown in a moderate oven.

CAVIAR D'AUBERGINES

Ingredients

2 eggplants	salt and pepper
2 cloves garlic	juice of a lemon
¼ cup chopped parsley	2 oz olive oil

Put the eggplants close to the grill until the skin turns black and is slightly charred. Plunge them into cold water for 2 or 3 minutes and peel. Mince the flesh together with the garlic. Add parsley, lemon juice and seasoning. Then stir in the olive oil, a little at a time. If there is any surplus, drain this off. Serve very cold.

AUBERGINES AU FOUR
(baked eggplants)

Ingredients

2 eggplants	juice and grated rind of a lemon
1 large pepper	1 large tomato
1 oz olive oil	2 shallots
cupful of breadcrumbs	3 anchovy fillets

Wash and slice the unpeeled eggplants. Fry in the olive oil together with the chopped shallots and tomato. Remove from heat and add the anchovy fillets, lemon juice and rind and the pepper, having first removed seeds and chopped small. Put into a well-greased ovenproof dish, top with the breadcrumbs, sprinkling a little olive oil over them. Bake 40 minutes in a moderate oven, or until well browned.

AUBERGINES A LA BOURGUIGNONNE

Ingredients

2 eggplants	3 oz mushrooms
2 shallots	1 egg
1 clove garlic	seasoning

Cut the washed eggplants into halves and remove the pulp. Fry the skins together with the finely chopped garlic, shallots and mushrooms. Season. Stir in the well-beaten egg. Stuff the eggplant skins with this mixture and put in an ovenproof dish having first covered the bottom with olive oil. Bake 40 minutes in a moderate oven.

BEIGNETS D'AUBERGINES
(eggplant fritters)

Ingredients

2 eggplants	½ pint milk
1 egg	¼ cup chopped parsley
2 oz flour	seasoning

Make a batter by putting the flour and seasoning into a bowl and making a well in the centre. Break egg into this and beat well. Add gradually the milk. Cover with a cloth and leave in a warm place for 2 hours. Wash the eggplant and slice. Leave to drain. Dip the eggplant slices in the batter mixture and fry in deep fat. Sprinkle with the parsley on serving.

AUBERGINES FARCIES
(stuffed eggplants)

Ingredients

2 eggplants	2 oz mushrooms
3 tbsp olive oil	1 egg
4 shallots	¼ pint tomato *coulis*
1 clove garlic	(see page 188)

Cut the eggplants, well washed, into halves and remove pulp. Fry the skins together with the sliced shallots, mushrooms and garlic, in 2 tbsp of the olive oil. In a bowl mix the eggplant pulp with the fried vegetables and well-beaten egg. Stuff the skins of the eggplants with this mixture and place in an ovenproof dish, having covered the bottom with 1 tbsp of olive oil. Bake in a moderate oven for 3 minutes and serve with the tomato *coulis.*

AUBERGINES EN SOUFFLÉ

Ingredients	sauce
2 eggplants	3 eggs
½ pint *béchamel*	2 oz grated cheese

Wash the eggplants, cut in halves and fry lightly. Remove the pulp, chop finely and mix with the *béchamel,* the egg yolks and the cheese. Add the well-whipped egg whites, return to skins and put in a well-greased ovenproof dish. Bake 20 minutes in a hot oven.

FENOUIL AU BEURRE

Ingredients	4 oz butter
4 fennel stems	seasoning

Scrub well the fennel and split each stem into quarters. Put in a pan together with the butter, seasoning and half a pint of water. Cover and simmer for 40 minutes.

FENOUIL AU JUS

Ingredients	3 tbsp of the juices in
4 fennel stems	which a joint of meat
	has been roasted

Prepare the fennel and boil in salted water for 30 minutes. Drain and return to pan with the meat juices. Simmer 10 minutes.

FENOUIL EN SALADE
(fennel salad)

Ingredients	salt and pepper
2 fennel stems	half a cup chopped parlsey
2 tbsp olive oil	1 tbsp chopped basil
1 tbsp vinegar	pinch of mustard

Thoroughly scrub the fennel, remove outer leaves, cut the hearts into small pieces and put into salad bowl. Toss well with a dressing made from mixing together the olive oil, vinegar, seasoning and herbs.

GRATIN DE FENOUIL
(baked fennel)

Ingredients

4 fennel stems	2 eggs
2 oz butter	2 oz grated Parmesan
1 pint milk	cheese
1 tbsp flour	salt and pepper

Prepare the fennel, removing hard outer leaves, and boil in salted water for 20 minutes. Drain and return to pan with the butter on low heat for 5 minutes. Now add the milk, a little at a time, and simmer a further 20 minutes. Stir in the flour. Allow to cool and add the Parmesan cheese and well-beaten eggs. Put in a greased ovenproof dish. Put this in a larger one containing water (the *bain-marie* method) and bake in a moderate oven for 20 minutes.

POIVRONS EN SALADE
(salad of sweet peppers)

Ingredients

2 red peppers	tsp chopped shallot
2 tbsp olive oil	¼ cup chopped parsley
1 tbsp vinegar	16 black olives

Boil the peppers until tender, cut in halves and remove core and seeds. Drain and arrange on a dish in flat, petal shapes. Cover with the olive oil and parsley. Sprinkle with the shallot and garnish with the olives.

POIVRONS EN GELÉE
(sweet peppers in aspic)

Ingredients

2 red peppers	1 shallot
1 cup tomato purée	pinch of mustard powder
2 tbsp olive oil	¼ tsp vinegar
1 oz powdered gelatine	seasoning
	1 egg yolk

Cut peppers in halves, remove core and seeds and boil 5 minutes in salted water. Dissolve the gelatine in a little hot water and when on the point of setting add to the tomato purée. Fill peppers with this and serve, very cold, with the mayonnaise made as follows. Break the egg yolk into a bowl with the mustard powder and beat, then add the oil, drop by drop, beating all the time until a creamy consistency is obtained. Add the vinegar and seasoning.

POIVRONS FARCIS
(stuffed sweet peppers)

Ingredients

2 green peppers	juice of a lemon
½ cup finely chopped parsley	salt and pepper
	1 breakfastcup rice
1 tbsp chopped basil	2 tbsp olive oil

Cut peppers in halves, removing core and seeds. Boil the rice fast for 8 minutes and drain. Put in a bowl with the parsley, basil, seasoning, lemon juice and 1 tbsp of the olive oil. Stuff the peppers with this mixture. Cover the bottom of an ovenproof dish with the remaining olive oil. Put in the peppers. Cover and bake half an hour in a slow oven.

POIVRONS AUX AMANDES
(sweet peppers with almonds)

Ingredients

2 green peppers	2 tbsp olive oil
1 small white cabbage	½ oz butter
cupful of slivered almonds	seasoning

Boil the peppers until tender. Cut in halves, removing core and seeds. Fry the shredded cabbage in the butter. Season. In a separate pan lightly fry the almonds until golden. Stuff the peppers with the cabbage. Sprinkle with the almonds and heat through in the oven.

AVOCATS A LA FRANÇAISE
(avocado pear appetizer)

Ingredients	juice of half a lemon
2 avocado pears	pinch of Cayenne pepper
dsp olive oil	tbsp chopped tarragon

Cut the pears in halves and remove stones. Scoop out the flesh, taking care not to pierce the skins, and mash well with the olive oil, lemon juice, Cayenne pepper and tarragon. Return to shells and refrigerate.

AVOCATS FARCIS
(stuffed avocado pears)

Ingredients	2 oz Roquefort or other
2 avocado pears	blue cheese
2 tbsp mayonnaise	½ tsp vinegar

Cut the pears in halves and remove stones. Scoop out the flesh and mix with the mayonnaise, well-crushed Roquefort and vinegar. Return to skins and refrigerate.

AVOCATS AU FOUR
(baked avocado pears)

Ingredients	1 pint of peeled shrimps
2 avocado pears	2 tbsp tomato purée

Cut the pears in halves and remove stones. Scoop out the flesh and mash well with the tomato purée. Mix in the shrimps, return to skins and put these in an ovenproof dish. Add water to half way up the skins and bake 30 minutes in a moderate oven.

8

MUSHROOMS

Field mushrooms are the best known of edible fungi, the most important others being morels, chanterelles, truffles and boletus.

Although a number of varieties are to be found in the woods, it is unsafe to pick them except with a specialist's knowledge, apart from the easily recognizable field mushroom. These mushrooms should be rose beneath the caps. If this has turned black they should be discarded.

Field mushrooms are, of course, ideal for the Englishman's favourite dish of mushrooms on toast. The French cultivated variety are seldom served like this, but there are many other ways of using them as a supper dish. They also make a good hors d'oeuvre and are excellent for soup.

Moreover, those to whom they seem expensive need buy only a small quantity, sufficient to transform quite ordinary dishes into something special, as well as using them for garnishing, sauces and adding to the fillings of omelettes, flans, pies, *vol-au-vents* and canapés.

There is no need to peel mushrooms. To scrub and wash them well in very hot water (this to bring out the flavour) is all that is necessary. Nor should the stalks be discarded since they are perfectly adequate for introducing the subtle flavour of mushrooms into a dish.

Served *à la crème* or *en purée* they make a good accompaniment for fish, meat or poultry, while baked they go well with a roast.

They should be used as fresh as possible. If not used immediately they should be plunged into boiling water for two minutes and they can then be safely kept for several days. When included in a stew or other meat or fish dishes it is preferable to cook them separately and to add them during the last five minutes.

Girolles (or chanterelles) can be used in the recipes given for *cèpes* (or boletus) and are particularly to be recommended in omelettes. They can be found, usually dried, in specialist grocers, delicatessens and big stores.

So, too, can *morilles* (or morels) which have a particularly delicate flavour. When the dried variety are used they should be soaked in tepid water for several hours, changing the water occasionally.

Truffles are a parasitic kind of mushroom which grow underground on the roots of oak-trees and are snuffed out by pigs and dogs.

There are a number of varieties of which the most appreciated are those from the region of Périgord. Actually 70 per cent now come from the Vaucluse further south but since those produced there are the species known as the *truffe du Périgord* they are equally costly, fetching around £25 the pound in the market and considerably more in the shops, since they travel badly. Which is why they are known as 'black diamonds'.

It is hoped, however, that eventually prices will fall since the French Institute of Agronomic Research is working on ways to make their production automatic.

It is on account of their exorbitant price and their penetrating scent that they are used largely for flavouring. They are excellent for stuffing turkey and pork. As a dish on their own, however, they are quite exquisite and have been known since antiquity, being mentioned in Roman feasts.

When dried, they should be soaked for several hours before using and will keep for up to a week.

CHAMPIGNONS EN SALADE
(raw mushroom salad)

Ingredients

1 lb mushrooms	2 oz cream
cupful chopped parsley	juice of a lemon
olive oil	seasoning

Scrub well the mushrooms, slice and leave to soak in the olive oil for about 2 hours, turning occasionally. Set on a plate and mix well with the cream, lemon juice and seasoning. Sprinkle with the parsley.

CHAMPIGNONS A LA GRECQUE

Ingredients

¼ lb button mushrooms	cupful finely chopped
½ pint white wine	parsley
bouquet garni	seasoning

Well scrub the mushrooms and discard the stalks. Cook the heads in the wine together with the *bouquet garni* and seasoning until tender. Leave until cold. Remove *bouquet garni* and sprinkle with the chopped parsley.

CHAMPIGNONS EN AMUSE-GUEULE
(mushroom cocktail)

Ingredients

¼ lb button mushrooms	2 oz tomato ketchup
2 oz cream	tsp Worcester Sauce
2 oz mayonnaise	tbsp chopped chives
	seasoning

Discard the stalks and scrub well the mushrooms. Boil for 2 minutes. Drain and mix with the cream, mayonnaise, Worcester Sauce, ketchup and seasoning. Put into individual glasses, sprinkle with the chives and refrigerate.

CHAMPIGNONS A LA CRÈME

Ingredients

1 lb mushrooms	pinch of nutmeg
2 oz olive oil	½ cup chopped parsley
seasoning	2 shallots
	3 oz cream

Scrub well the mushrooms, slice and lightly fry in the olive oil. Add the chopped shallots, seasoning and nutmeg and cook a further 2 minutes. Stir in the parsley and cream and serve immediately.

CHAMPIGNONS GRILLÉS
(grilled mushrooms)

Ingredients
4 large mushrooms
salt and pepper

1 oz olive oil
1 oz butter
½ cup chopped parsley

Scrub the mushrooms, removing stalks. Season, sprinkle with the olive oil and put under a hot grill for 10 minutes. Melt the butter, add the parsley and, on serving, fill the mushroom cavities with this.

CHAMPIGNONS SAUTÉS AUX FINES HERBES
(fried mushrooms)

Ingredients
1 lb mushrooms
2 tbsp chopped parsley
2 garlic cloves
1 tbsp chopped tarragon

1 tbsp chopped chives
2 oz butter
juice of half a lemon
salt and pepper

Scrub well the mushrooms, slice and fry gently in the butter together with the garlic, parsley, tarragon and seasoning. Add the chives and lemon juice on serving.

CHAMPIGNONS A LA TUNISIENNE

Ingredients
½ lb button mushrooms
juice of half a lemon
bouquet garni

2 tbsp tomato *coulis*
(see page 188)
seasoning
1 oz olive oil

Remove the stalks and fry the well-scrubbed mushrooms in the olive oil for 2 minutes. Add the lemon juice, *bouquet garni*, tomato *coulis* and seasoning. Bring to the boil and simmer for 10 minutes. Serve cold, removing the *bouquet garni* before serving.

CHAMPIGNONS EN SOUFFLÉ

Ingredients

¼ lb mushrooms	1 oz flour
2 eggs	½ pint milk
2 oz butter	pinch of nutmeg
	¼ cup chopped parsley

Melt 1 oz of the butter, stir in the flour and then, gradually, the milk. Stir until it thickens. Allow to cool, then beat in the egg yolks. Lightly fry the chopped mushrooms in the remaining butter, season, and add together with the nutmeg and parsley to the sauce. Lastly fold in the egg whites whisked until stiff. Put into a well-buttered soufflé dish. Put this into a pan of water and bake 20 minutes in a hot oven until well risen and golden.

CHAMPIGNONS EN PURÉE

Ingredients

1 lb mushrooms	pinch of nutmeg
1 oz flour	2 oz butter
seasoning	2 oz cream

Boil the mushrooms in sufficient water to cover. Drain, preserving the liquid and sieve the mushrooms. Melt 1 oz of the butter, stir in the flour and add, gradually, the cooking water. Add the sieved mushrooms, nutmeg, seasoning and cream. Re-heat, stirring in the remaining ounce of butter.

CHAMPIGNONS FARCIS
(baked stuffed mushrooms)

Ingredients

4 large mushrooms	seasoning
¼ cup chopped parsley	1 tbsp olive oil
1 egg	breadcrumbs

Scrub well the mushrooms. Remove stalks and chop these with the parsley. Add the beaten egg and seasoning. Stuff the mushroom cavities with this, top with the breadcrumbs and put into an ovenproof dish, having covered the bottom with olive oil. Bake in a moderate oven until tender.

CHAMPIGNONS EN COQUILLES

(mushrooms in scallop shells)

Ingredients

1 lb mushrooms	yolks of 2 eggs
½ pint milk	cupful breadcrumbs
3 oz butter	juice of half a lemon
1 oz flour	salt and pepper

Scrub and slice the mushrooms and boil, just covered with water, for 5 minutes. Drain. Make a sauce by melting 2 oz of the butter, stirring in the flour and then, gradually, the milk. Stir until it thickens. When cool, whisk in the egg yolks, then add the mushrooms, lemon juice and seasoning. Put into scallop shells, sprinkle with the breadcrumbs and dot with the remaining butter. Bake in a hot oven until golden.

MATELOTE DE CHAMPIGNONS

(mushrooms in red wine)

Ingredients

1 lb button mushrooms	2 shallots
1 oz butter	4 garlic cloves
¾ pint red wine	salt and pepper
1 tbsp cognac	*bouquet garni*

In the red wine simmer the *bouquet garni*, shallots and unpeeled garlic cloves for 20 minutes. Remove the *bouquet garni*, shallots and garlic and add the mushrooms (having discarded the stalks). Simmer 5 minutes, then boil fast until only about a cupful of wine is left. Add the cognac and stir in the butter, a little at a time.

CHAMPIGNONS EN CROÛTE

Ingredients

½ lb mushrooms	1 oz flour
juice of half a lemon	3 oz butter
margarine	4 pieces of bread, about 3
seasoning	inches thick, cut from
	a French loaf

Scoop out the crumb from the pieces of bread, leaving about half an inch at the bottom of each. Lightly fry the sliced mushrooms in the butter. Add lemon juice and seasoning. Now make a sauce by melting the remaining ounce of butter, stirring in the flour and adding, gradually, the milk. Stir until it thickens. Add the mushrooms and keep warm. Fry the *croûtes* in the margarine and fill with the mushroom mixture.

CÈPES AU VIN BLANC
(chanterelles in white wine)

Ingredients
1 lb chanterelles
2 cloves garlic
½ pint white wine
½ oz butter
seasoning

Scrub well the chanterelles, discarding the stalks. Insert a piece of garlic into each and simmer in the wine for 20 minutes. Add the butter and seasoning and stir for a further 2 minutes.

CÈPES A LA BORDELAISE

Ingredients
1 lb chanterelles
2 oz olive oil
1 shallot
¼ cup chopped parsley
juice of half a lemon

Remove the stalks from the well-scrubbed chanterelles and chop. Fry together with the sliced shallots in the olive oil for 2 minutes on each side. Lower heat and cook gently for 5 minutes. Fry again quickly for 2 minutes (this to prevent their becoming flabby). Drain off any surplus oil. Add the lemon juice and sprinkle with the parsley.

CÈPES AU GRATIN
(baked chanterelles)

Ingredients
1 lb chanterelles
2 oz olive oil
1 cup browned
　breadcrumbs
½ pint white wine

Fry the chanterelles with the shallot, as in previous recipe. Pour off any surplus oil and add the white wine and seasoning. Put into ovenproof dish, top with the breadcrumbs and bake 10 minutes.

CÈPES PÉRIGOURDINE

Ingredients
4 large chanterelles
3 cloves garlic
2 shallots

½ lb mushrooms
¼ cup chopped parsley
juice of half a lemon
seasoning

Mince the well-scrubbed mushrooms and mix with the chopped garlic, shallots, parsley, seasoning and lemon juice. Grill the chanterelles, spread with a little olive oil, for 5 minutes on each side and put in an oiled ovenproof dish. Cover with the mushroom mixture and bake 15 minutes in a moderate oven.

CÈPES EN FRICASSÉE

Ingredients
1 lb chanterelles
2 oz butter
1 tbsp flour
½ pint milk
bouquet garni

½ pint stock or dissolved
   meat cube
salt and pepper
1 egg
juice of a lemon

Slice the well-scrubbed chanterelles and fry slowly in the butter with the *bouquet garni* and seasoning for 20 minutes. Remove *bouquet garni,* stir in the flour and stock and simmer a further 5 minutes. Remove a little of the liquid and mix this with the well-beaten egg. Return to pan, add the lemon juice and serve immediately.

MORILLES SAUTÉES
(fried morels)

Ingredients
1 lb morels
2 oz butter
few drops lemon juice

salt
pepper
pinch of nutmeg

Wash the morels very quickly by plunging them into a basinful of water and drying in a cloth. Slice and fry in the butter with the lemon juice, seasoning and nutmeg, for 20 minutes. Add, on serving, a tablespoonful of the cooking juices from a roast.

MORILLES A LA PROVENÇALE

Ingredients

1 lb morels	2 oz olive oil
2 onions	salt
3 cloves garlic	pinch of Cayenne pepper

Prepare the morels and ‘boil for 10 minutes. Drain. Lightly fry the sliced onions and garlic in the butter, add the morels and seasoning and continue cooking a further 5 minutes.

MORILLES A LA CRÈME

Ingredients

1 lb morels	¼ pint stock or meat cube
2 oz butter	¼ pint cream
juice of half a lemon	seasoning

Cook the prepared morels in 1 oz of the butter together with the lemon juice, stock and seasoning, until tender. In a separate pan melt the remaining 1 oz of butter and stir in the cream. Add to the morels but do not allow to boil.

TRUFFES EN GARNITURE

(truffles to serve with a roast of meat or poultry)

Ingredients

¼ lb truffles	seasoning
2 oz butter	juice of half a lemon

Wash the truffles, cleaning with a hard brush if fresh. Peel and put in pan with the butter, seasoning and lemon juice. Simmer 3 minutes. Add sufficient of the juices from a roast to cover and simmer a further half-hour.

TRUFFES SOUS LA CENDRE

Ingredients
¼ lb truffles   4 bacon rashers

Prepare the truffles and wrap in the bacon rashers. Wrap again in oiled paper, closing well. Cook for half an hour under a pile of hot ashes in a wood fire. If this is not possible, bake three-quarters of an hour in a moderate oven.

TRUFFES AU CHAMPAGNE

Ingredients   2 oz veal stock
¼ lb truffles   1 oz butter
glassful of champagne   salt and pepper

Prepare the truffles and put into a pan with the butter and wine. Boil 5 minutes. Add the champagne and seasoning and simmer a further 15 minutes.

9

OLIVES AND CHESTNUTS

The cultivation of the olive dates back to antiquity, being sanctified in the Bible as a symbol of peace and abundance, while Hebrew law forbade it to be cut down. As far back as 2500 B.C. the forests of Crete were being replaced by olive groves. They enriched the Greeks and Romans who planted them in north Africa.

The tree is very adaptable owing to its tough endurance and system of roots. It will not grow, however, above 400 metres in altitude nor in a temperature below -8°C.

Its importance, of course, was that it was the source of an oil that was indispensable not only for food but to burn lamps, as the basis of medicine and for the unction of priests and kings. It was already well known in Greece in the sixth century B.C. since laws were enacted regarding its cultivation. It was the Greek colonists who carried it westwards to become thoroughly naturalized throughout the Mediterranean region where the ritual wine and bread with a handful of olives has been the diet of the poor since earliest times.

Olives are particularly nourishing and digestible, containing iron, vitamins and non-saturated fat.

It is thought that the olive tree was responsible for the nomadic tribes of the Middle East settling down and planting the slow maturing trees, which live up to a thousand years, for the benefit of their children and grandchildren. The Phoenicians introduced the olive into Spain which, with Italy, is the biggest producer in the world.

In France the olive groves, with their silvery evergreen leaves, fragrant flowers and gnarled trucks and roots, symbolize the countryside of Provence. There are a number of varieties which are gathered, green and unripe, in October, while those left to ripen on the trees, when they become black, are gathered in January.

It is these that are used for the oil which is obtained by expression from the pulp of the fleshy fruit. During nearly two thousand years the means of this extraction was a stone press, but almost everywhere now this is being replaced by machines. In times past the gathering of the olives was the occasion for festivities such as those which still accompany the grape harvest.

There are several pressings, producing oil of varying quality and the connoisseur, especially in Provence, is very particular about the kind of olive oil he uses, for it provides the fat in which everything is cooked as well as for the dressing of salads.

Both black and green olives are preserved in brine. When bought loose they should be packed into screw-top jars, covered with olive oil and stored in the refrigerator.

Black ones are generally used for cooking, in *pizzas*, *salade nicoise* and in stews. Green olives, however, are used for the cooking of poultry as in the famous *canard aux olives*. They are used, too, as hors d'oeuvres, stuffings, sauces and garnishing.

Much less is known about the origins of the chestnut which is believed to have been introduced into Sardinia from Asia Minor and from there to have spread all over Europe.

Chestnuts are highly nutritive and in some regions where they are particularly abundant, such as Corsica, they are used for flour which serves to make their *polenta,* whereas in Italy maize flour is used.

For those on a diet chestnuts have the double advantage of containing only a minimum amount of salt and yet, owing to their particularly savoury flavour, have no need for any seasoning.

When required for a purée the round variety are better, being more floury.

To facilitate peeling, they should be scored across and boiled for about ten minutes. Only a few at a time should be taken out of the water since it is easier to deal with them while hot. A sharp knife should be used in order to remove both shell and skin at the same time.

There are many ways of using them other than the traditional roasting in the embers and as stuffing for turkey.

In France chestnut purée accompanies wild boar and goes well, too, with roast pork and as a stuffing for red cabbage. When boiled, they are excellent mixed with brussels sprouts. They make a delicious soup and have many uses in confectionery, such as *marrons glacés* although the preparation of these is such a lengthy one that they are nearly always produced commercially.

OLIVES FARCIES (1)
(stuffed olives)

Ingredients
2 dozen large green olives, de-stoned if possible

2 anchovy fillets
2 oz butter
pepper

De-stone the olives if this has not already been done and fill with the anchovy fillets, chopped and well pounded with the butter and pepper.

OLIVES FARCIES (2)

Ingredients
2 dozen large green olives
small tin of tunny fish

1 oz butter
2 oz capers
pepper

Prepare olives as above and stuff with the tunny fish pounded with the butter and capers. Add pepper.

OLIVES FARCIES (3)

Ingredients
2 dozen large green olives

2 oz smoked salmon
½ cup breadcrumbs
juice of half a lemon

Prepare the olives as above. Soak the breadcrumbs in water, squeeze out and add to the chopped salmon and the lemon juice. Stuff the olives with this.

FARCE D'OLIVES
(olive stuffing)

Ingredients

20 black olives	1 garlic clove
small cupful stale bread	tbsp chopped parsley
1 shallot	1 egg

Soak the bread in water and squeeze out. Add to the de-stoned and well-chopped olives together with the parsley and well-crushed shallot and garlic. Beat in the egg and blend well.

RAGOÛT D'OLIVES
(stewed olives)

Ingredients

4 oz green olives	1 tsp chopped chives
1 oz butter	1 tsp chopped parsley
¼ pint white wine	1 soupspoon olive oil
1 oz flour	1 anchovy fillet
	1 soupspoon capers.

Melt the butter and add the parsley, chives, white wine and ¼ pint water. Simmer 2 minutes. Add the de-stoned olives and the flour. Proud the anchovy fillet in the olive oil and add, together with the capers. Serve to accompany poultry.

CANAPÉS MÉRIDIONAUX

Ingredients

20 black olives	garlic salt
gherkins	rounds of toast or rye
2 oz butter	bread

Soften the butter and pound with the de-stoned olives and the garlic salt. Spread on the canapés and top each with a slice of gherkin.

TAPENADE

Ingredients

20 black olives	**2 oz capers**
2 oz tunny fish	**pepper**
2 oz olive oil	**juice of half a lemon**

De-stone the olives and pound to a purée with the anchovy fillets, tunny fish and capers. Add the olive oil, drop by drop, stirring all the time. Lastly add the pepper and lemon juice. Serve either on canapés, in pastry barques or as a stuffing for hardboiled eggs, in which case the yolks should be pounded into the tapenade.

OLIVES ÉPICÉES
(spiced olives)

Ingredients

black olives as required	**dried orange peel**
thyme	**olive oil**

Put the olives in a jar together with the thyme and orange peel. Fill up with the olive oil, cover hermetically and shake daily for 20 days, when they will be ready for consumption.

PURÉE DE MARRONS
(chestnut purée)

Ingredients

1 lb chestnuts	**milk**
2 oz butter	**seasoning**

Score the chestnuts and boil 10 minutes. Remove shells and skin. Cover with the milk, simmer until soft and sieve. Return to pan with the seasoning and butter. Heat through.

MARRONS ÉTUVÉS
(steamed chestnuts)

Ingredients

1 lb chestnuts	**4 celery sticks**
	¼ pint consommé

Score the chestnuts and boil for 8 minutes. Peel, being careful to keep them whole. Steam, together with the consommé and chopped celery, over a pan of boiling water.

MARRONS RÔTIS
(roast chestnuts)

Ingredients
chestnuts as required

Prick the chestnuts in several places with a fork and roast in embers or in a frying pan over a gentle heat.

CROQUETTES DE MARRONS

Ingredients	**pepper**
1 lb chestnuts	**1 oz butter**
few grains fennel	**flour**

Boil the chestnuts 8 minutes. Remove skins and sieve. Blend in the butter, pepper and fennel seeds. Form into balls, roll in the flour and fry in deep fat until golden.

GÂTEAU DE MARRONS
(chestnut cake)

Ingredients	
1 lb chestnuts	**few drops vanilla essence**
1 pint milk	**1 oz cornflour**
4 oz sugar	**1 oz chocolate powder**
1 egg	**½ oz butter**

Score the chestnuts and boil 10 minutes. Remove skins and sieve. Add half a pint of the milk, vanilla, 2 oz of the sugar and the egg. Make a caramel by boiling together the remaining 2 oz of sugar in a little water. Coat an ovenproof dish with this and pour in the chestnut mixture. Bake 30 minutes in a moderate oven or until, when inserting a knife, it comes out clean. Serve with a chocolate sauce made by melting the butter, stirring in the cornflour and then, gradually, the remaining half pint of milk. Stir until it thickens.

CRÈME DE MARRONS

Ingredients

1 lb chestnuts
few drops vanilla essence
a few walnuts and a tbsp
   of honey

cupful mixed hazel nuts
   and almonds both well
   ground

Boil the chestnuts 8 minutes and remove skins. Return to pan a further 5 minutes with a cupful of water and the vanilla essence. Sieve, reserving the cooking water. Blend in the honey, ground hazel nuts and almonds. Serve in individual glasses, decorating with the walnuts.

MARRONS AU MIEL

(chestnuts with honey)

Ingredients

1 lb chestnuts

cupful honey
1 oz kirsch

Prick the chestnuts and put on a tray in the oven. Cover with the honey and heat just long enough to heat the honey. Sprinkle with kirsch, flame and pour over the chestnuts. Serve immediately.

MOUSSE DE MARRONS

Ingredients

1 lb chestnuts
2 oz sugar
2 oz butter
2 oz cream

½ pint milk
4 eggs
few drops of vanilla
   essence

Score the chestnuts, boil 10 minutes and skin. Return to pan with the milk, butter and vanilla, bring to the boil and simmer until tender. Add sugar and sieve. Fold in the egg yolks and the cream. Whip well the whites and add. Serve very cold.

COMPOTE DE MARRONS

Ingredients
1 lb chestnuts

cupful honey
1 oz kirsch

Score the chestnuts, boil 10 minutes and skin. Make a syrup with the sugar and water. Add the chestnuts and simmer for 10 minutes. Add the rum and serve immediately.

SOUFFLÉ AUX MARRONS

Ingredients
½ lb chestnuts
3 eggs

½ pint milk
1 oz butter
seasoning

Score the chestnuts, boil 10 minutes and skin. Return to heat with the milk and simmer until tender. Sieve and stir in the butter, egg yolks and seasoning. Whip the whites until stiff and add. Put into a well-buttered soufflé dish and bake 20 minutes in a hot oven until well risen.

CONFITURE DE MARRONS

(chestnut jam)

Ingredients
2 lb chestnuts

3 lb sugar
tsp vanilla essence

Score the chestnuts, boil 10 minutes and peel. Return to pan with a pint of water and simmer until tender. Sieve. Put this purée into a large pan. In a separate pan dissolve the sugar in a pint of boiling water, add the vanilla essence and simmer 10 minutes. Add, a little at a time, this syrup to the chestnuts. Bring to the boil and simmer 20 minutes, or until set when tested. Pour into previously prepared jars and seal in the usual way.

10

THE ONION FAMILY

Onions, Leeks and Garlic

Most indispensable of *les aromates*, the flavouring vegetables, the onion has been grown since earliest times. The Egyptians regarded it as sacred, considering it a link between man and eternity so that it was buried with them as a kind of currency to pay their way through the difficult passages of the netherworld. In certain regions, such as Afghanistan, it still grows wild.

It was Alexander the Great who introduced the onion into Europe, and Louis Pasteur who, in 1858, discovered that onion juice completely stops the development of lactic fermentation, but that after boiling it loses its harmful action on microbes.

Its strong taste and smell are due to a volatile oil rich in sulphur which is supposed to induce sleep. It is a powerful diuretic, is good for sufferers from diabetes and kidney complaints and calms the pain of rheumatism. When eaten raw, however, it is indigestible.

It also contains a considerable quantity of glucose, and it is this which, when processed, can be turned into onion essence. It is perhaps also the reason why supposedly any dish that takes onion will also take apple and that the French add apples to their stews.

Its other uses are to put a halved one in the refrigerator to remove smells and into the water when boiling mussels. If it turns black it is an indication that there is a bad mussel in the pan.

To avoid shedding tears one should peel them over a basin of cold water, while after use it is advisable to plunge the knife into cold water before washing it in hot.

Many varieties of onion have been established by selection. The Spanish onion is popular on account of its comparatively mild flavour. The Welsh onion, or *ciboule,* is a native of Siberia from where it was introduced early in the seventeenth century. It never forms a bulb but is very hard.

When buying, choose ones that are firm. They can be stored for several months and are good to eat so long as they do not begin to sprout.

When frying, a sprinkling of sugar enables them to brown quickly. When boiling, they should be pricked to keep them whole. They can also be roasted in the same way as potatoes.

Spring onions make an excellent hors d'oeuvre, go well in salads and can be preserved in vinegar. When mature, they are excellent in soups and stews, the popular French onion soup being particularly satisfying.

They can be eaten on their own too, either boiled or roasted. When boiled, thirty minutes' cooking completely assures their digestibility. Before putting into stews they should first be browned. To soften them without browning a little olive oil should be added to the butter.

The violet-tinted shallot which originated in Palestine is a small variety of onion. Its uses are the same but it is considered more digestible.

Leeks, which have a far milder flavour than onions, were greatly esteemed by the ancient Egyptians and Romans, the latter being thought to have introduced them into Britain. Like onions they are diuretic. An essential ingredient of vegetable soups, there are many other ways of serving them as well.

When buying, choose those with as much white and little green as possible. To clean, they should be slit from the top to about half way down and then held under running water to remove all grit.

The British seem at last to be overcoming their prejudice over garlic, although in fact it is only when eaten raw that the flavour is offensive. For those, however, who would freshen the mouth after a dish which contains raw garlic, the chewing of coffee beans is considered good.

In France, which is the biggest consumer of garlic in

Europe, it is considered particularly good for the circulation of the blood, while the lift it gives to certain dishes is irreplaceable.

The French always fry it with their steak and insert a clove into roasts of lamb and beef. It goes well, too, with baked fish. It is an essential to an *aioli* sauce, so popular in the Midi, to their Provençal cod dish of *bourride* and for stuffing snails.

A small garlic crusher is a particularly useful gadget, but rubbing round a dish with a clove can be sufficient to impart its delicate flavour.

Garlic was known to the ancient Egyptians since it is recorded on an inscription on one of the pyramids of Gizeh that a distribution of garlic cloves was made to the labourers in order to ward off illness and brace them for their tasks.

The plant consists of a bulb, called the head, containing small bulblets, known as cloves. Garlic salt, which is extracted from this, is useful for flavouring. Another subtle way of flavouring with garlic is to use it unpeeled. Like this a large quantity can be used to stuff birds, as well as to flavour soups and meat dishes, and removed before serving.

Never use garlic which is old and has turned yellow as it can be toxic. When frying, never allow to brown or it will become bitter.

For those who possess a garden, chives are very useful. They grow quickly and the grass-like leaves can be snipped off with scissors for flavouring and garnishes. Before using, it is best to remove all the little mauve flower-buds.

OIGNONS DE PRINTEMPS EN HORS D'OEUVRE
(hors d'oeuvres of spring onions)

Ingredients
1 lb small spring onions
2 oz raisins
breakfastcupful of tomato
   coulis (see page 188)
1 tsp vinegar
pinch of Cayenne pepper
2 tbsp olive oil
tsp salt
bouquet garni

Put together in pan the tomato *coulis*, vinegar, olive oil, Cayenne and salt. Blend well, then add the peeled onions, raisins and *bouquet garni*. Simmer 1 hour, turning occasionally to prevent sticking and, if necessary, adding a little water. Leave to cool, refrigerate and remove *bouquet garni* before serving.

OIGNONS GLACÉS
(glazed onions)

Ingredients

1 lb small spring onions	3 oz butter
¼ pint consommé or stock	2 oz sugar

Melt the butter, add sugar and the peeled onions and turn for a few minutes until yellow. Add the consommé and boil fairly fast, so that the liquid reduces, and spooning it over the onions until they begin to caramelize. Serve as a garnish.

OIGNONS CONFITS
(pickled onions)

Ingredients

1 lb small spring onions	2 bayleaves
1 tsp peppercorns	pinch of nutmeg
wine vinegar	2 chillies

Put the peeled onions in a pan with the bayleaves, peppercorns, nutmeg and chillies. Cover with the vinegar, bring to the boil and simmer 20 minutes. Refrigerate well in order to prevent the onions turning flabby before pouring into preserving jars.

OIGNONS A LA GRECQUE

Ingredients

¼ lb small spring onions	cupful finely chopped
¼ cup white wine	parsley
bouquet garni	seasoning

Peel the onions and simmer in the wine together with the *bouquet garni* and seasoning until tender. Leave until cold. Remove *bouquet garni* and sprinkle with the chopped parsley.

PURÉE D'OIGNONS

Ingredients	salt and pepper
1 lb onions	pinch of nutmeg
milk	2 oz butter

Put the peeled onions in a pan with the seasoning and nutmeg and cover with equal parts milk and water. Simmer until well cooked. Sieve and return to pan with the butter, blending well.

OIGNONS A LA CRÈME

Ingredients	2 oz cream
4 large onions	1 egg
2 oz butter	2 rashers streaky bacon

Peel the onions, cut into quarters and put in an oven-proof dish together with the butter. Bake in a moderate oven until golden, then add the chopped bacon rashers. Cook a further 10 minutes. Allow to cool, then mix with the well-beaten egg and the cream. Return to oven for a further 5 minutes.

OIGNONS RÔTIS
(cold baked onions)

Ingredients	1 dsp vinegar
4 large onions	salt and pepper
2 tbsp olive oil	¼ cup chopped parsley

Put the unpeeled onions in an ovenproof dish with a little water and bake in a moderate oven until tender. Remove skins and serve, cold, with the French dressing made by mixing together the olive oil, vinegar, seasoning and parsley.

OIGNONS BRAISÉS
(braised onions)

Ingredients	1 tbsp cooking juices from
1 lb onions	a roast
2 slices streaky bacon	salt and pepper

Peel the onions and put in an ovenproof dish or a saucepan together with the chopped bacon, seasoning and meat juices. Cover and cook gently until tender.

OIGNONS FARCIS
(stuffed onions)

Ingredients	1 egg
4 large onions	seasoning
2 cloves garlic	1 oz butter
¼ cup chopped parsley	browned breadcrumbs

Peel the onions, cutting off the base in order that they stand firmly and boil until just tender. With a sharp knife remove the inner part, chop small and mix with the parsley, seasoning, crushed garlic and well-beaten egg. Stuff the onion shells with this mixture and put in an ovenproof dish. Sprinkle with the breadcrumbs and dot with the butter. Bake 20 minutes.

OIGNONS EN COQUILLES
(onions in scallop shells)

Ingredients	
½ lb onions	¼ pint milk
1 oz flour	seasoning
3 oz butter	white breadcrumbs

Peel and slice the onions and put in a pan with water to cover. Simmer until tender. Drain, saving the cooking water. Melt 2 oz of the butter, stir in the flour and add, gradually, the milk and ¼ pint of the cooking water. Season and stir until it thickens. Butter the scallop shells and put a little of the sauce into each, heap the prepared onions on this and cover with the remaining sauce. Sprinkle with the breadcrumbs and dot with the butter. Bake until well browned.

OIGNONS EN SOUFFLÉ

Ingredients

¼ lb onions	1 oz flour
3 eggs	pinch of nutmeg
2 oz butter	seasoning

Peel the onions, boil until tender and sieve, pressing out all surplus water. Melt the butter, stir in the flour and add the cooking onions. No liquid is necessary. Season and blend well. Allow to cool and add the egg yolks. Then fold in whites whisked until stiff. Put into a well-buttered soufflé dish and bake 25 minutes in a hot oven, or until well risen and golden.

OIGNONS EN PÁTÉ
(onions in batter)

Ingredients

1 lb onions	seasoning
2 oz flour	½ pint milk
1 egg	1 oz butter

Peel and boil the onions until tender. Drain and mash roughly. Make a batter by putting the flour and seasoning into a bowl and making a well in the centre. Break egg into this and beat well. Add, gradually, the milk. Cover with a cloth and stand in a warm place for 2 hours. Put the butter in an ovenproof dish, turn up the oven and when butter has melted put in the onions and then the batter mixture. Bake 40 minutes in a hot oven, or until well risen.

BEIGNETS D'OIGNONS
(onion fritters)

Ingredients

3 large onions	batter mixture as for
¼ cup chopped parsley	above recipe

Prepare the batter as above. Peel the onions, slice in rings and drain on kitchen paper. Dip in the batter mixture and fry in deep fat. Sprinkle with the parsley on serving.

TARTE A L'OIGNON

Ingredients

¼ lb onions

short pastry (2 oz butter
   to 5 oz flour)

1 oz butter

2 eggs

2 oz grated cheese

10 stoned black olives

2 oz cream

·Prepare pastry and place in an 8-inch flan tin. Bake blind until firm but not golden. Peel and slice the onions and fry lightly in the butter until yellow. Remove from heat and add the well-beaten eggs, cream and seasoning. Cover flan with this, sprinkle with the cheese and dot with the olives. Bake a further 10 minutes in a moderate oven.

TERRINE D'OIGNONS
(baked onions)

Ingredients

1 lb onions

seasoning

¼ lb mushrooms

2 garlic cloves

1 large tomato

browned breadcrumbs

1 tbsp olive oil

Peel and lightly fry the onions. Put in a well-buttered ovenproof dish and cover with a tomato sauce made by heating the olive oil and in it frying the chopped garlic and mushrooms. Add the crushed tomato and cook a further 2 minutes. Top with the breadcrumbs and bake 15 minutes in a moderate oven.

OIGNONS A LA REINE

Ingredients

4 large onions

bouquet garni

cloves

¼ pint Madeira wine

1 oz flour

2 oz butter

tsp capers

seasoning

Insert a clove into each onion and put these in a pan with the *bouquet garni*. Cover with water and boil until tender. Add the Madeira wine and drain, saving the liquid. Serve with a sauce made by melting the butter, stirring in the flour and then adding, gradually, the liquid from the onions. Season and add capers.

OIGNONS AU VIN ROUGE
(onions in red wine)

Ingredients
1 lb onions
red wine
bouquet garni

bouillon or dissolved
   meat cube
salt and pepper
2 oz olive oil

Peel and slice the onions and cook gently in the olive oil until yellow. Cover with equal parts wine and bouillon, add seasoning and *bouquet garni* and simmer until tender. Then boil fast until liquid is reduced and syrupy. Remove *bouquet garni* and serve as accompaniment to a roast.

OIGNONS AU VIN BLANC
(onions in white wine)

Ingredients
1 lb small spring onions
1 pint white wine
juice of a lemon
salt and pepper

1 large tomato
tsp coriander seeds
2 oz sultanas
2 bayleaves
2 oz olive oil

Peel and slice the onions and cook gently in the olive oil until yellow. Add the lemon juice, crushed tomato, sultanas, seasoning, bayleaves, coriander seeds, and wine. Bring to the boil and simmer 45 minutes. Then boil fast to reduce to a syrup. Refrigerate and remove *bouquet garni* before serving.

OIGNONS LYONNAIS

Ingredients
1 lb onions
½ oz flour, stock
1 oz butter

bouquet garni
pinch of nutmeg
2 eggs
seasoning

Hardboil the eggs and remove shells. Peel and slice the onions and cook gently in the butter until yellow. Stir in the flour, moisten with a little of the stock and add nutmeg, seasoning and *bouquet garni*. Simmer 20 minutes. Remove *bouquet garni*, add the sliced hardboiled eggs and heat through.

OIGNONS AUX MARRONS
(onions with chestnuts)

Ingredients	milk
1 lb onions	½ oz flour
½ lb chestnuts	seasoning
2 rashers streaky bacon	1 oz butter

Score and boil the chestnuts 9 minutes. Remove shells and skins. Peel and slice the onions and simmer in the milk for 10 minutes. Add the chopped chestnuts and simmer a further 10 minutes. Drain, saving the milk. Cut up the bacon rashers small and fry gently in the butter. Add the onions, chestnuts and seasoning. Stir in the flour and heat through.

OIGNONS FRITS (1)
(fried onions)

Ingredients	
1 lb onions	browned breadcrumbs
1 egg	seasoning
2 tbsp milk	olive oil

Peel the onions and cut into rings. Beat well the egg and add milk and seasoning. Dip the onion rings first in the flour, then in the egg and milk and lastly in the breadcrumbs. Fry in the olive oil until golden.

OIGNONS FRITS (2)

Ingredients	
2 large onions	4 oz flour
2 oz margarine	olive oil

Peel the onions and chop small. Mix the softened margarine with the flour until crumbly. Add sufficient water to make a firm consistency. Add the onion. Roll out, cut into rounds and fry in the olive oil.

OIGNONS EN CANAPÉS

Ingredients

¼ lb onions	nutmeg
rounds of toast	yolks of 2 eggs
1 oz butter	salt and pepper
¼ oz flour	1 oz grated cheese

Peel the onions and boil until tender. Drain and sieve, reserving the liquid. Make a sauce by melting the butter, stirring in the flour and adding, gradually, the milk. Season and stir until it thickens. Add the onions and spread on the toast. Top with the grated cheese and bake until golden.

POIREAUX EN SALADE
(leek salad)

Ingredients

8 large leeks	1 tsp vinegar
1 oz olive oil	salt and pepper

Thoroughly wash the leeks, discarding green part, and boil 20 minutes in salted water. When cold, dress with the well-mixed olive oil, vinegar and seasoning.

POIREAUX GRATINÉS

Ingredients	1 oz flour
8 large leeks	salt and pepper
2 oz butter	browned breadcrumbs

Prepare the leeks and boil 20 minutes in salted water. Drain, saving the water, and put in an ovenproof dish. Make a white sauce by melting the butter, stirring in the flour and adding, gradually, ½ pint of the cooking water. Stir until it thickens and season. Cover the leeks with this sauce. Sprinkle with the breadcrumbs and bake 10 minutes.

POIREAUX BRAISÉS
(braised leeks)

Ingredients
8 medium-sized leeks
seasoning

4 tbsp of the juices from
a roast

Prepare the leeks, discarding the green part, and cut into lengths of about 2 inches. Put in a pan together with the seasoning and meat juices, cover and simmer very slowly for 1 hour.

POIREAUX AU FOUR
(baked leeks)

Ingredients
8 large leeks
2 oz butter
1 breakfastcup fresh
    breadcrumbs

½ oz flour
½ pint milk
seasoning
2 oz grated cheese

Prepare the leeks, discarding the green part and mix with the breadcrumbs previously soaked in milk and squeezed out. Put in an ovenproof dish. Make a sauce by melting the butter, stirring in the flour and then the milk and seasoning. Pour this fairly liquid sauce over the leek and bread mixture. Bake in a slow oven, basting fairly often with the sauce until the leeks are tender. Sprinkle with the cheese, turn up the heat and continue cooking until golden.

FLAMICHE AUX POIREAUX
(leek flan)

Ingredients
1 lb leeks
1 oz flour
4 oz butter
2 oz breadcrumbs

½ pint milk
short pastry (2 oz butter
    to 5 oz flour)
seasoning
yolk of an egg

Prepare pastry, put into 8-inch flan tin and bake blind until firm but not golden. Prepare the leeks, discarding the green part. Cut into small pieces and fry gently in 2 oz of the butter until soft. Make a sauce by melting 1 oz of butter, stirring in the flour and adding, gradually, the milk. Stir until it thickens. Off the heat add the well-beaten egg yolk and seasoning. Mix with the leeks and cover the flan. Top with the breadcrumbs and dot with the remaining ounce of butter. Bake 20 minutes.

POIREAUX MAINTENANT

Ingredients

1 lb leeks	**seasoning**
2 oz butter	*croutons* **(small squares**
1 oz flour	**of stale bread fried**
1 pint rosé wine	**in butter)**

Prepare the leeks, chop and cook gently in the butter until soft. Stir in the flour and add the seasoning and wine. Simmer 40 minutes and serve with the *croûtons*.

BOULETTES DE POIREAUX
(leek rissoles)

Ingredients

4 large leeks	**2 eggs**
1 oz grated cheese	**flour**
seasoning	**olive oil**
	1 lemon

Prepare the leeks and boil half an hour. Drain and sieve. Mix with the cheese, seasoning and well-beaten eggs. Form into balls, roll in the flour and fry in the olive oil, turning so that they are well browned but soft inside. Serve with the lemon juice.

POIREAUX A LA GRECQUE

Ingredients

1 lb small leeks	*bouquet garni*
½ cup chopped parsley	**seasoning**
	½ pint white wine

Prepare the leeks, discarding green part, and cut into 2-inch pieces. Put these in a pan with the wine, *bouquet garni* and seasoning and simmer until tender. Leave until cold. Remove *bouquet garni* and sprinkle with the parsley.

POIREAUX A LA PROVENÇALE

Ingredients

1 lb leeks	juice and well-chopped
2 oz olive oil	rind of a lemon
2 tomatoes	cupful stoned black olives

Prepare the leeks, chop and put in a pan with the olive oil and seasoning. Cook gently until soft. Add the well-crushed tomatoes, the lemon rind and juice and the olives. Cook further 10 minutes.

POIREAUX FERMIER
(leeks farmhouse fashion)

Ingredients

½ lb leeks	1 pint chicken stock
2 shallots	cupful cream
2 medium-sized potatoes	¼ cup mixed herbs, as
2 oz butter	available

Prepare the leeks discarding green part, chop small and fry together with the peeled and sliced shallots in the butter until soft. Add the chopped potatoes, stock and seasoning and simmer until all the vegetables are cooked. Drain and sieve. Return to pan with the cream, blend well and sprinkle with the well-chopped herbs on serving.

POIREAUX AU VIN ROUGE
(leeks in red wine)

Ingredients

1 lb leeks	consommé or meat stock
2 oz olive oil	seasoning
2 garlic cloves	breakfastcupful fresh
red wine	breadcrumbs
salt and pepper	1 oz butter

Prepare the leeks and chop the white part only. Cook in the olive oil together with the garlic cloves until soft, being careful not to allow the garlic to brown. Cover with part red wine and part consommé, add seasoning and simmer 10 minutes. Turn up heat to reduce liquid. Transfer to an ovenproof dish, sprinkle with the breadcrumbs, dot with the butter and bake 15 minutes in a moderate oven.

FROTTE D'AIL
(garlic bread)

Ingredients
4 garlic cloves
1 French loaf

2 oz olive oil
cupful minced olives
salt

Cut the loaf into 4 equal-sized pieces. Split down the centre and rub each side with the garlic cloves until well imbibed. Fill with the minced olives and season to individual taste.

TOAST A L'AIL
(garlic toast)

Ingredients
8 slices cut from a
   sandwich loaf

4 garlic cloves
salt and pepper

Mince the garlic, season and spread on 4 pieces of the buttered bread slices. Sandwich with the remaining slices and bake in a moderate oven until crisp.

L'AIL AU FOUR
(baked garlic)

Ingredients
garlic as required

fresh French bread
cream cheese

Peel the garlic cloves and put in a well-greased ovenproof dish. Bake until they begin to brown, then add a cupful of water and cook a further half-hour, basting every 10 minutes. Serve with the bread and cream cheese.

CROÛTES D'AIL

Ingredients

4 pieces of bread, about 2 inches thick, cut from a French loaf

6 garlic cloves

cupful black olives

4 anchovy fillets

2 oz butter

½ cup chopped parsley

Scoop out the crumb from the pieces of bread, leaving about half an inch at the bottom of each. Pound together the garlic, stoned olives and chopped anchovy fillets. Blend well with the softened butter. Put this mixture into a saucepan while the bread is frying in deep fat. Drain the bread, fill with the garlic mixture and top with the parsley.

OEUFS À L'AIL
(garlic eggs)

Ingredients

4 eggs

6 cloves garlic

2 anchovy fillets

tbsp capers

dsp paprika

½ oz olive oil

juice of half a lemon

Hardboil the eggs and shell. Cut in halves. Crush well the garlic and add to the chopped anchovy fillets and egg yolks. Blend in the paprika, olive oil and lemon juice and fill egg whites with this mixture.

BEURRE D'AIL
(garlic butter)

Ingredients

6 garlic cloves

4 oz butter

salt and pepper

Pound the garlic and blend with the softened butter, salt and pepper. Refrigerate before using to stuff snails, etc.

11
PULSES

Pulses are those vegetables in which it is the seeds that are edible, the best known of which are peas. Of these there are two main varieties, the garden and field, together with an immense number of sub-varieties.

Their origin is unknown, although it is supposed from their ancient cultivation that they are indigenous to Europe and western Asia. They were first brought to France from Italy and were later extremely popular at the court of Louis XIV. *Canard aux petits pois* (duck with fresh peas) was soon to become a popular dish and has remained so ever since.

They were introduced into England through France and Holland in the early sixteenth century, but a hundred years elapsed before they were grown and appreciated as a table vegetable.

Few vegetables have become more improved during the past century as regards quality and productivity. When buying, choose those that are very green. They should be shelled just before cooking, being one of the vegetables which lose their flavour most easily. When buying them tinned, the products of France and Belgium are the most natural, containing no colouring matter and little sugar. When frozen they are as good as fresh.

Any dish described as *St. Germain* indicates that a purée of green peas is included.

Dried, they take the form of split peas, particularly appreciated in soups and purées.

Pea-beans, called realistically in French *mange-tout*, are a special variety in which the pods are eaten as well as the

peas. Choose those that are very green, discarding any that
are yellow.

The grain or chick pea belongs to a different species from
the field and garden peas. For long particular to Spain and
Italy, it is now grown in southern France as well. With a
somewhat strange flavour it is an essential ingredient of
couscous, a hot dish from Morocco and Algeria, of which
there are numerous restaurants in France. It is also good in
soups and salads.

A long soaking and cooking is necessary, with the addition of a pinch of bicarbonate of soda.

All dried pulses, in fact, need soaking although if this is
too long there is a risk of fermentation so that it is wise to
change the water every few hours. The length of time
depends on their freshness. If they are more than a year old
a pinch of bicarbonate of soda should be added.

White haricot beans and broad beans are, technically
speaking, also pulses. But they have already been included
in the chapter on beans.

Lentils are one of the most important pulses of various
Eastern countries and a staple item of cultivation. They have
been grown since Biblical times, mention of them being
made in Genesis.

The small, dark green ones which become brown when
cooked are the best buy, the other varieties quickly
becoming mushy when boiled so that they are really only
suitable for soups and purées. Unlike white haricot beans,
they are very digestible.

Great care should be taken to remove any small stones,
not easily discernible since they are the same colour as the
lentils. The best way is either to spread them out on the
table and pick them over, or else drop them in small
quantities on to a plate when the sound of a stone is immediately noticeable.

Soya is also a pulse which has been grown since earliest
times in the extreme Orient where it is the germs of the
seeds that are eaten. Soya oil has for long been used in
France but the seed germs have become popular recently,
making a delicious and refreshing salad. Like all pulses, it
is of great nutritive value.

PETITS POIS A LA FRANÇAISE

Ingredients
1 lb peas
½ pint water
salt and pepper

2 shallots
heart of a lettuce
½ oz butter
½ oz sugar

Put the peas in a saucepan with the water, shallots, lettuce and seasoning. Boil until tender. Remove shallots and lettuce and add the sugar and butter. Shake a few seconds more before serving.

PETITS POIS AU BEURRE

Ingredients
1 lb peas
1 oz salt

· 2 oz butter
dsp sugar

Put the peas in a pan with the sugar, salt and just sufficient water to cover. Bring to the boil and simmer 20 minutes. Return to pan with the butter and cook a further 2 minutes, turning well.

PURÉE DE PETITS POIS

Ingredients
1 lb peas
¼ cup chopped parsley
2 shallots

1 tsp sugar
salt and pepper
1 oz butter

Put the peas in a pan with the parsley and shallots. Cover with hot water, bring to the boil and simmer until tender. Remove the parsley and shallots. Sieve the peas and return to pan with the butter, sugar and seasoning. Simmer a further 2 minutes.

PETITS POIS A LA CRÈME

Ingredients
1 lb peas
2 oz butter
¼ cup chopped parsley

2 onions
2 oz cream
salt and pepper

Put the peas in a pan with the butter and cook a few minutes, turning constantly. Add the sliced onions, parsley, seasoning and a breakfastcup of water. Cover and simmer until tender. Then boil fast so that only about 1 tbsp of liquid remains. Stir in the cream and serve immediately.

PETITS POIS AU JUS

Ingredients	2 shallots
1 lb of peas	tsp each of sugar and salt
heart of a lettuce	2 tbsp juices from a roast

Put the peas in a pan with the lettuce, shallots, salt and sugar. Add sufficient hot water to cover and cook until tender. Drain and return to pan with the meat juices. Simmer a further 2 minutes.

PETITS POIS BONNE FEMME

Ingredients	¼ cup chopped parsley
1 lb peas	salt and pepper
10 small onions	2 oz butter
2 bacon rashers	1 oz sugar
1 small lettuce	1 oz flour

In the butter lightly fry the onions and diced bacon until soft. Add the peas, the shredded lettuce, parsley, sugar and seasoning. Add just sufficient hot water to cover. Cover and boil until tender. Mix the flour with a little of the cooking water and stir in. Blend well.

PETITS POIS A LA FLAMANDE
(peas Flemish style)

Ingredients	tsp sugar
1 lb peas	2 oz butter
¼ lb carrots	salt

Clean and scrape the carrots, cut into rounds and put in a pan with 1 oz of the butter, sugar, salt and sufficient water to cover. When half cooked add the peas and cook a further 20 minutes. Add the remaining butter.

PETITS POIS AU RIZ
(peas with rice)

Ingredients

1 lb peas	salt and pepper
2 garlic cloves	1 oz olive oil
breakfastcup water	2 oz rice

Put the peas in a pan with the chopped garlic cloves, seasoning and water. Cover and simmer slowly until tender. Add the rice and cook fast until cooked (about 8 minutes). Stir in the olive oil and blend well.

PETITS POIS EN SALADE
(salad of green peas)

Ingredients

1 lb peas	pinch of mustard powder
breakfastcup rice	salt and pepper
½ pint shrimps	tsp vinegar
1 egg yolk	olive oil

Boil the rice fast for 8 minutes and drain. Cook the peas with a pinch of bicarbonate of soda (to keep them green) until tender. Drain. Make a mayonnaise by putting the egg yolk in a bowl with the mustard and beating well. Add the olive oil, drop by drop, beating all the time until a creamy consistency is obtained. Add the vinegar and seasoning. Mix this mayonnaise with the peas and rice. Put in a mould and turn out when cold. Garnish with the shelled shrimps.

PETITS POIS EN MATELOTE

Ingredients

1 lb peas	2 bacon rashers
juice of half a lemon	1 oz butter
3 artichoke hearts	breakfastcupful stock
8 small onions	or bouillon cube

Put the peas in a pan with the sliced artichoke hearts, the chopped bacon rashers, the butter and lemon juice. Cover with the stock and simmer 40 minutes. Add seasoning at the end of the cooking.

POIS MANGE-TOUT A L'ÉTOUFFE

(steamed pea-beans)

Ingredients

1 lb pea-beans	2 shallots
2 bacon rashers	pinch of nutmeg
1 lettuce	salt and pepper
	tsp sugar

Prepare the pea-beans by plunging into hot water and then slicing. Line the top of a double boiler with the bacon rashers and put in the other ingredients. Cover and steam over boiling water until tender.

POIS MANGE-TOUT EN TOURTIÈRE

(pea-beans in the oven)

Ingredients

1 lb pea-beans	salt and pepper
tbsp chopped chives	2 oz butter
pinch of grated nutmeg	breakfastcupful stock or
2 cloves	dissolved bouillon cube
tbsp mixed herbs	2 tbsp juices from a
	roast

Prepare the pea-beans and put in a pie-dish with the chives, cloves, herbs, butter, seasoning and stock. Cover and cook in a slow oven until tender. Sprinkle with the nutmeg, add the meat juices and continue cooking a further 5 minutes.

PURÉE DE POIS CASSÉS

(purée of split peas)

Ingredients

½ lb split peas	*bouquet garni*
2 oz butter	salt and pepper

Soak the peas several hours. Drain, cover with fresh water and simmer until tender, together with the *bouquet garni*. Remove *bouquet garni*. Force peas through vegetable mill and return to pan with the butter and seasoning. Blend in sufficient of the cooking water to make it the consistency of a purée. Heat through.

POIS CASSÉS AUX OEUFS
(split peas with eggs)

Ingredients
¼ lb split peas
4 eggs
4 bacon rashers

croûtons (small squares of stale bread fried in butter)

Prepare and cook the peas as in previous recipe. Sieve and put in an ovenproof dish. Lightly fry the eggs and bacon rashers. Cover the peas with these, top with the *croûtons* and bake 10 minutes in a moderate oven.

POIS CASSÉS A LA FERMIERE
(split peas farmhouse style)

Ingredients
¼ lb split peas
2 eggs
2 oz butter

sprig of thyme and a bay-leaf
salt and pepper
1 oz cream

Soak the peas and cook together with the thyme and bayleaf in a minimum of water until tender. Remove thyme and bayleaf and force peas through vegetable mill. Return to pan with the seasoning, cream, butter and well-beaten eggs. Heat through, blending well.

POIS CHICHES A LA ROMAINE

Ingredients
¼ lb chick peas
2 ripe tomatoes

garlic salt
cupful chopped parsley
bouquet garni

Soak the chick peas for 24 hours. Put in pan, cover with cold water and a pinch of bicarbonate of soda and boil 20 minutes. Drain and put into boiling water with the *bouquet garni* and garlic salt. Simmer until tender. Drain off all but a little of the water, remove *bouquet garni* and stir in the crushed tomato and parsley.

POIS CHICHES EN SALADE
(salad of chick peas)

Ingredients	1 tsp vinegar
1 lb chick peas	1 shallot
bouquet garni	salt and pepper
2 tbsp olive oil	$\frac{1}{4}$ cup chopped parsley

Produce as for previous recipe, cooking until tender. Drain and when cold mix well with the olive oil, vinegar, seasoning and well-chopped shallots. Sprinkle with the parsley. If preferred, the skins can be removed before mixing with the French dressing.

POIS CHICHES AU FENOUIL
(chick peas with fennel)

Ingredients	2 cups chopped fennel
$\frac{1}{4}$ lb chick peas	(including stalks)
2 garlic cloves	1 large tomato
sprig of thyme	$\frac{1}{4}$ lb mushrooms
pinch of Cayenne pepper	1 onion
salt	2 oz olive oil

Prepare the peas and cook until tender. Drain, reserving the water. Heat 1 oz of the olive oil and lightly fry the fennel and chopped garlic cloves, stirring all the time. Add the peas, Cayenne, salt, thyme and water to moisten. Simmer 10 minutes. Serve with a tomato sauce made by lightly frying the sliced onion and mushrooms in the remaining ounce of olive oil. Blend in the well-crushed tomato.

LENTILLES A LA MAÎTRE D'HÔTEL

Ingredients	$\frac{1}{2}$ cup finely chopped
1 lb lentils	parsley
1 oz butter	salt and pepper

Pick over the lentils to make sure there are no stones. Soak if necessary. Cook in salted water until tender and drain. Melt the butter and add the lentils, parsley and seasoning. Turn for a few minutes and serve immediately.

LENTILLES AU JUS

Ingredients
1 lb lentils
¼ cup chopped parsley

1 shallot
2 tbsp juices from a roast
seasoning

Prepare the lentils as above. Boil until tender and drain. Put the meat juices in a pan with the parsley, seasoning, well-chopped onion and meat juices. Simmer 5 minutes. Add the lentils and cook a further 5 minutes.

LENTILLES AU BLANC
(lentils with white sauce)

Ingredients
1 lb lentils
1 oz butter

½ oz flour
tbsp chopped parsley
seasoning

Proceed as in above recipe. Drain the lentils, saving the cooking water. Make a white sauce by melting the butter, stirring in the flour and then, gradually, half a pint of the cooking water. Stir until it thickens. Add the parsley and lentils and heat through.

LENTILLES EN PURÉE

Ingredients
1 lb lentils
½ pint milk

2 oz butter
seasoning

Proceed as in above recipe. Drain the lentils and force through vegetable mill. Return to pan with the butter and seasoning, adding the milk a little at a time. Blend well.

LENTILLES EN SALADE
(lentil salad)

Ingredients
1 lb lentils
1 shallot
2 tbsp olive oil

1 tbsp vinegar
tsp mustard powder
salt and pepper
1 shallot

Proceed as in above recipe. Drain the lentils and while still warm dress with the well-mixed olive oil, vinegar, mustard, seasoning and chopped shallot. Refrigerate.

LENTILLES AU LARD

Ingredients

1 lb lentils	¼ lb small onions
¼ lb smoked pork or	1 oz butter
streaky bacon	1 tbsp flour

Prepare the lentils and put in pan with a minimum of water together with the pork or bacon, cut small, and the onions. Simmer until tender. Drain, saving a little of the water. Melt the butter, stir in the flour and a cupful of the cooking water. Add the lentils and the diced pork or bacon and heat through.

LENTILLES AUX FINES HERBES
(lentils with herbs)

Ingredients

1 lb lentils	1 tbsp each of chopped
1 tsp cumin seeds	sage, mint, parsley and
dsp vinegar	basil
1 tsp pepper	pinch of saffron

Prepare the lentils and boil with the pepper and cumin seeds. When nearly cooked pour off all but a little of the water and finish cooking with the addition of the vinegar, herbs and saffron.

CROQUETTES DE LENTILLES

Ingredients	seasoning
½ lb lentils	¼ cup chopped parsley
2 chopped shallots	1 tomato
1 oz butter	2 garlic cloves
1 egg	¼ lb mushrooms
browned breadcrumbs	1 oz olive oil

Prepare the lentils, boil until tender and drain. Blend in the butter, parsley and seasoning and form into balls. Roll first in the flour, then in the beaten egg and lastly in the breadcrumbs. Fry until each side is golden. Serve with a sauce made by lightly frying the chopped garlic and mushrooms in the olive oil. Stir in the crushed tomato and simmer a further few minutes.

GERMES DE SOYA EN SALADE

(soya salad)

Ingredients

¼ lb germs of soya   1 tbsp lemon juice
2 tbsp olive oil   salt and pepper

Wash the soya germs and boil 2 minutes. Drain. When cold, dress with the olive oil, lemon juice and seasoning.

12

POTATOES

In France, potatoes, like other vegetables, are customarily served after the meat or fish as a separate course. For this reason, except when new, they are seldom boiled. They are also used frequently for soup and as supper dishes.

Whether or not they are included on the menu at all depends largely on the region. In the north of France they are considered as essential an item of the diet as in Britain.

The potato originated in South America from where the Spaniards brought it to Europe in the fifteenth century. But in France the prejudice against potatoes lasted for three centuries, it being thought, at first, that they caused leprosy and, when that accusation was proved absurd, that they caused fever.

In 1771, however, the Besançon Academy of Medicine ran a competition for the answer to the question: 'What plants can be used to supplement other foods in times of famine?' A military apothecary named Parmentier competed and proved that the potato was quite harmless.

Prejudice against it continued, however, despite potatoes now holding an important place on the menu, until Louis XVI had the inspiration of appearing in public wearing in his buttonhole Parmentier's 'little mauve flower', thus glorifying it in the eyes both of the court and of the people themselves.

It should be remembered that the leaves and green parts of the plant are poisonous, and that if potatoes are exposed to the light for a long time they assume a deep green colour and become unsafe to eat as they can contain the poison solanine.

As well as carbohydrates they also contain vitamin C, protein and mineral salts. The proteins are to be found in the layer just beneath the skin, so that they should always be peeled after boiling. Small potatoes, possessing as they do most skin area, are therefore more nutritious than larger ones.

Cooking in salted water is supposed to destroy much of the calcium content so that it is preferable to add the salt after the cooking.

To prevent boiled ones from breaking, the saucepan can be lined with newspaper, while it is easier to peel them when hot if held in a cloth.

When mashing, remember that to obtain a really smooth purée they are best forced through a vegetable mill or sieved before beating in the milk, butter and seasoning.

When cooked in their skins, either boiled or baked, they are commonly described in French as – *robe de chambre,* a corruption of the original *robe des champs* (of the fields) meaning in their skins as they were grown.

Like all apparently simple things, fried potatoes are often badly done. The easiest method is to deep-fry them in a wire basket so that they can be easily drained. A better flavour is obtained by frying them in olive oil, as well as their being less greasy. The addition of a bayleaf also improves the flavour. Whether preferred cut lengthwise (as chips), in wafer thin rounds (as crisps) or parboiled first (sautéed), they should be well dried in a cloth and not be put into the fat or oil until it is sizzling hot. They should be crisp, golden and served the moment that they are ready.

When no wire basket is available, chips can be fried in olive oil in a frying pan, with a little chopped garlic. This is a more tedious method, however, since they need to be frequently turned and draining is less satisfactory.

Most countries have their own version of baked potatoes, probably because they make such a good supper dish, and that of France, with herb-spiced cheese, is delectable.

Of all French potato dishes, *gratin dauphinois* and *gratin savoyard* are probably the best known, while *pommes dauphine, pommes duchesse* and *pommes lyonnaises* are equally good either to accompany meat or on their own.

PURÉE DE POMMES DE TERRE (1)

Ingredients
10 medium-sized floury
   potatoes

2 oz butter
¼ pint boiling milk
seasoning

Parboil the potatoes and peel. Return to pan and continue cooking until tender. Drain, force through vegetable mill and return to pan, stirring in the butter, milk and seasoning. Whip over heat to a light purée.

PURÉE DE POMMES DE TERRE (2)

Ingredients
10 medium-sized floury
   potatoes

seasoning
4 tbsp of the juices from a
   roast

Parboil the potatoes and skin. Return to pan and continue cooking until tender. Drain, force through vegetable mill and return to the pan with the seasoning and meat juices. Whip over heat to a light purée.

POMMES DUCHESSE

Ingredients
10 medium-sized floury
   potatoes
4 oz butter

2 tbsp self-raising flour
3 eggs
pinch of grated nutmeg
seasoning

Proceed as in recipe 1 for potato purée. Then melt the remaining 2 oz of butter, stir in the flour until smooth and remove from heat. Beat in the eggs, the nutmeg and seasoning and add to the potato purée blending thoroughly. Form into balls, the size of a large walnut, and drop into deep fat, turning until golden all over.

POMMES LYONNAISES

Ingredients
8 medium-sized potatoes
3 oz butter
4 shallots

seasoning
½ cup finely chopped
   parsley

Boil the potatoes, peel and slice. Fry gently in 2 oz of the butter until golden. In a separate pan lightly fry the sliced onions until yellow. Add to the potatoes together with the seasoning. Serve sprinkled with the parsley.

POMMES DE TERRE EN ALLUMETTES

Ingredients
potatoes as required

Peel the potatoes and cut into strips the size of a matchstick. Put into cold water for 10 minutes, drain and dry in a cloth. Fry in deep fat until golden.

POMMES DE TERRE FONDANTES

| *Ingredients* | **3 oz butter** |
| **1 lb small floury potatoes** | **tsp salt** |

Peel the potatoes and put into a pan sufficiently large for the potatoes to cover the bottom in one layer. Add salt, 1 oz of the butter, and water to half cover the potatoes. Cover hermetically and cook in a moderate oven. When the water is completely absorbed add the remaining butter and continue cooking until the potatoes are lightly browned.

POMMES DE TERRE A LA CRÈME

Ingredients	
1 lb new potatoes	**2 oz cream**
salt and pepper	**1 oz butter**

Scrape the potatoes and boil 20 minutes. Drain and return to pan with the butter and seasoning. Blend in the cream and serve immediately.

POMMES DE TERRE CHÂTEAU

Ingredients	
1 lb small new potatoes	**4 oz butter**
tsp sugar	**½ cup chopped chervil**
	salt

Scrape the potatoes and cook slowly in the butter together with the salt and sugar. Sprinkle with the chervil on serving.

POMMES DE TERRE AU VIN BLANC
(potatoes in white wine)

Ingredients

1 lb small potatoes	seasoning
2 bacon rashers	¼ pint white wine
1 oz butter	¼ pint meat stock or
2 bayleaves	dissolved meat cube

Put the potatoes in pan with the other ingredients and simmer until tender.

POMMES BONNE FEMME

Ingredients

1 lb potatoes	cupful mixed herbs
seasoning	2 oz cream
cupful chopped chives	2 egg yolks
and shallots	3 oz butter

Peel the potatoes, slice in thin rounds and fry in the butter until golden. Remove from the pan and replace with the cream, egg yolks, herbs, shallots and chives and seasoning. Stir well and pour over potatoes.

POMMES DE TERRE AU LAIT
(potatoes in milk)

Ingredients

1 lb potatoes	seasoning
milk	pinch of grated nutmeg
	4 oz butter

Boil the potatoes until tender. Peel and slice. Put in pan, cover with milk and add seasoning and nutmeg. Boil fast, stirring all the time, until the milk has reduced by two thirds. Off the heat, blend in the butter, a little at a time, and serve immediately.

POMMES DE TERRE EN ROBE DE CHAMBRE
(baked potatoes)

Ingredients

8 large floury potatoes   salt and pepper
                                 butter

Thoroughly scrub the potatoes and bake in their skins in a slow oven until cooked. Serve accompanied by salt and butter.

POMMES DE TERRE RÔTIES
(roast potatoes)

Ingredients

12 medium-sized potatoes   4 tbsp juices from a roast
4 oz butter   salt and pepper

Boil the potatoes 8 minutes. Drain, peel and cut in halves. Put in a tin with the butter and meat juices and roast in a moderate oven, turning occasionally, until golden. Sprinkle with salt and pepper on serving.

POMMES DE TERRE SAUTÉES

Ingredients

1 lb small potatoes   cupful well-chopped
seasoning   parsley

Parboil the potatoes and skin. Fry in deep fat until well browned and serve with the parsley and seasoning.

POMMES DE TERRE MAÎTRE D'HÔTEL

Ingredients

1 lb medium-sized   seasoning
    potatoes   cupful finely-chopped
4 oz butter   parsley

Boil the potatoes 10 minutes and drain. Peel and cut into slices. Lightly fry in the butter until golden on each side. Add the parsley and seasoning.

POMMES DE TERRE A LA LORRAINE
(savoury potatoes)

Ingredients
10 medium-sized potatoes
1 large onion
1 tbsp olive oil

1 tbsp butter
seasoning
bouquet garni
2 cups water

Peel and slice the potatoes. Slice onion and fry in the butter and oil until yellow. Add the potatoes, seasoning, *bouquet garni* and water. Simmer until tender. Remove *bouquet garni* before serving.

SALADE DE POMMES DE TERRE (1)
(potato salad)

Ingredients
10 medium-sized potatoes
2 tbsp olive oil
1 tbsp vinegar

seasoning
1 cup finely chopped
    parsley
2 shallots

Boil the potatoes until cooked but unbroken. Drain and peel. While still warm mix with the oil, vinegar and seasoning. Sprinkle with the finely chopped shallots and parsley and refrigerate.

SALADE DE POMMES DE TERRE (2)

Ingredients
1 lb potatoes
2 lettuce hearts
juice of half a lemon
2 oz olive oil

cupful stoned black olives
tsp capers
½ cup chives
seasoning

Shred the lettuce hearts. Boil the potatoes until cooked but unbroken. Drain and peel. Mix with the olive oil and lemon juice. Put the lettuce in a salad bowl together with the olives, capers and seasoning. Mix in the potatoes when cold and sprinkle with the chives.

POMMES DE TERRE EN GELÉE
(potatoes in aspic)

Ingredients
8 medium-sized potatoes
1 oz powdered gelatine
1 cup hot water
seasoning

2 finely chopped onions
juice of half a lemon
2 tbsp mayonnaise
1 tsp mustard powder
bunch of watercress

Proceed as in recipe (1) for potato purée. Dissolve the gelatine in the water. Add the other ingredients and, lastly, the potato purée. Put into a baking ring and refrigerate. Turn out, filling the centre with the prepared watercress.

GRATIN DAUPHINOIS

Ingredients
1 lb potatoes
1 pint milk
1 well-beaten egg
pinch of grated nutmeg

seasoning
2 oz butter
3 oz grated Gruyère
    cheese

Wash and peel the potatoes. Slice thinly and put into an ovenproof dish which has previously been rubbed round with a garlic clove. Mix together the milk, nutmeg, 2 oz of the grated cheese and the seasoning. Cover potatoes with this. Top with the remaining cheese and the butter chopped small. Bake 40 minutes in a moderate oven.

GRATIN SAVOYARD

Ingredients
1 lb potatoes
seasoning
half cupful parsley
2 oz butter

3 oz grated Gruyère
    cheese
pint of meat stock or
    chicken broth
1 egg

Proceed as in above recipe, with the addition of the parsley and replacing the milk by the stock or broth.

POMMES DE TERRE FARCIES
(stuffed potatoes)

Ingredients
8 medium-sized potatoes
2 shallots
2 cloves garlic

¼ lb mushrooms
2 oz butter
2 oz grated cheese
seasoning

Lightly fry the chopped mushrooms and garlic in the butter. Add seasoning. Well scrub the potatoes and bake in a slow oven until they begin to soften. Cut in halves. Scoop out the interior and mix with the mushrooms and garlic. Return to skins, top with the grated cheese and finish cooking until the cheese is well browned.

POMMES DE TERRE A LA PROVENÇALE

Ingredients
8 medium-sized potatoes
2 large ripe tomatoes

2 onions
1 oz olive oil
seasoning

Peel the potatoes, removing bottoms so that they stand upright on a greased plate. Bake 40 minutes. Lightly fry the sliced tomato and onions in the olive oil and add seasoning. Remove interior of the potatoes and mix with the tomatoes and onions. Fill the skins with this and return to oven for a further 10 minutes.

POMMES DE TERRE AUX FINES HERBES

Ingredients
8 medium-sized potatoes
1 oz cream cheese

cupful mixed herbs as
    available
seasoning

Scrub well the potatoes and bake in a slow oven until they begin to soften. Cut in halves. Remove interior and mix well with the cream cheese, herbs and seasoning. Return to skins and bake a further 20 minutes.

POMMES DE TERRE AU FOUR

(oven potatoes)

Ingredients
12 medium-sized potatoes	2 oz butter
2 eggs	1 oz olive oil
	seasoning

Parboil the potatoes, peel and slice. Spread the olive oil over the bottom of an ovenproof dish and put in the potatoes and seasoning. Top with the butter and cook in a slow oven until the potatoes begin to brown. Add the well-beaten eggs, increase the heat and continue cooking a further 10 minutes.

POMMES ALSACIENNES

(potatoes Alsacian style)

Ingredients
6 medium-sized potatoes	1 clove of garlic
2 oz flour	1 cup chopped parsley
2 eggs	½ tsp grated nutmeg

Boil and mash the potatoes. Add the other ingredients. Put in a well-buttered pie dish and bake 20 minutes.

CROQUETTES DE POMME DE TERRE

(potato balls)

Ingredients
4 large potatoes	yolks of 2 eggs
seasoning	2 oz butter
	2 oz olive oil

Scrub the potatoes and bake. When cooked, remove skins and force through vegetable mill. Add the butter, seasoning and beaten egg yolks. Blend well. When nearly cold, form into small balls, flattening top and bottom, roll in flour and fry in the olive oil until golden on both sides.

CROQUETTES SUCRÉES

(sweet potato balls)

Ingredients
1 lb potatoes	2 oz butter
2 eggs	2 oz sugar

Make a purée of the potatoes. Whip the eggs and add. Form into balls, flattening top and bottom. Roll in flour and fry in the butter. Drain. Sprinkle with the sugar and serve very hot.

POMMES DE TERRE AU FROMAGE
(cheese potatoes)

Ingredients	2 tbsp tomato *coulis*
8 medium-sized potatoes	(see page 188)
1 oz butter	cupful consommé
2 oz flour	2 oz grated cheese

Boil the potatoes. Drain and slice. Put in an ovenproof dish. Melt the butter, stir in the flour and add, gradually, the consommé. Blend in the tomato *coulis* and the grated cheese. And this sauce to the potatoes and bake 20 minutes in a moderate oven.

SOUFFLÉ DE POMMES DE TERRE

Ingredients	
½ lb floury potatoes	pinch of grated nutmeg
3 eggs	½ pint milk
2 oz butter	salt and pepper

Parboil the potatoes and skin. Finish cooking, drain and force through vegetable mill. Whisk in the milk, egg yolks, butter, nutmeg and seasoning. When cool, fold in the egg whites beaten until stiff. Put in a buttered ovenproof dish and bake 25 minutes in a hot oven until well risen and golden.

POMMES DE TERRE ANNA

Ingredients	2 oz butter
1 lb new potatoes	seasoning

Peel the potatoes, slice very thinly and put into cold water for 10 minutes. Drain and dry in a cloth. Butter an ovenproof dish and put in layers of the sliced potatoes, in overlapping rows. Dot with the butter, season and bake 1 hour in a moderate oven. To serve, invert the dish, draining off any surplus fat.

POMMES DE TERRE EN MATELOTE

Ingredients	½ pint red wine
1 lb potatoes	seasoning
3 oz butter	2 onions
1 dsp flour	*bouquet garni*

Peel and slice the potatoes. Slice the onions. Melt the butter and stir in the flour. Add ¼ pint water and the wine. Simmer 2 minutes. Add the potatoes, onions, seasoning and *bouquet garni* and cook half an hour. Remove *bouquet garni* before serving.

GALETTE DE POMMES DE TERRE

Ingredients	2 onions
10 medium-sized potatoes	3 oz butter

Boil the potatoes. Drain, peel and slice. Fry in the butter, together with the sliced onions and seasoning, pressing well down with a palette knife so that they cover the whole of the pan. Shake at intervals to prevent sticking. When a crust has formed, invert and serve immediately.

GÂTEAU PARMENTIER

Ingredients	2 oz butter
1 lb floury potatoes	seasoning
2 oz flour	4 bacon rashers

Boil the potatoes, drain and peel. Mash well, adding the flour, seasoning and butter. Put in a well-greased flan tin. Cover with the bacon rashers and bake half an hour. Turn out to serve.

OMELETTE PARMENTIER

Ingredients
4 medium-sized potatoes
4 eggs
2 bacon rashers

¼ cup finely chopped parsley
1 oz butter
salt and pepper

Parboil the potatoes, peel and cut into cubes. Fry in the butter together with the chopped bacon rashers until browned. Add parsley and seasoning. Make 4 omelettes and fill with the potato mixture.

CRÊPES DE POMMES DE TERRE

(potato pancakes)

Ingredients
4 medium-sized potatoes
2 oz flour
1 oz grated cheese

pinch of grated nutmeg
salt and pepper
half pint milk
1 onion

Peel the potatoes and grate. Lightly fry the sliced onion and mix with the raw sliced potatoes. Add seasoning, nutmeg, grated cheese and flour. Stir in the milk. Make pancakes in the usual way with the potato batter.

POMMES DE TERRE A LA BARIGOULE

Ingredients
1 lb medium-sized
   potatoes
meat stock
bouquet garni

2 tbsp olive oil
6 small onions
1 tbsp vinegar
salt and pepper

Peel the potatoes and put into pan with the *bouquet garni* and onions. Cover with the stock. Bring to the boil and simmer 30 minutes. Drain off the stock, add the olive oil, vinegar and seasoning and simmer a further 2 minutes.

BEIGNETS DE POMMES DE TERRE

(potato fritters)

Ingredients
4 medium-sized potatoes
1 egg

2 oz flour
¼ pint milk
2 oz butter

Make a batter by putting the flour in a bowl, making a well in the centre and into this break the egg. Blend well and add the milk, a little at a time. Now make a purée with the potatoes. Add this to the batter, beating in the butter. Form into balls the size of a large walnut and fry in deep fat. Drain well and sprinkle with either salt or sugar.

PATATE VOSGIENNE

Ingredients

8 medium-sized potatoes	flour
seasoning	2 oz grated cheese
2 oz cream	½ pint milk
1 egg	1 large onion

To a potato purée add the milk and seasoning. Blend in flour until a firm consistency. Roll out and put in a flan tin. Cover with the cream, the onion sliced into rings and the grated cheese. Bake 25 minutes in a hot oven.

BOULETTES
(potato dumplings)

Ingredients

1 lb potatoes	4 oz grated cheese
½ pint milk	1 egg
2 oz butter	flour
seasoning	½ pint tomato *coulis*

Boil the potatoes and mash with the milk, seasoning, cheese and 1 oz of the butter. Beat in the egg. Form into balls, roll in flour and drop into a pan of boiling water. They are cooked when they rise to the surface. Serve with a sauce made by melting the remaining ounce of butter and stirring in the tomato *coulis*.

GNOCCHI

Ingredients

¼ lb potatoes	1 egg
½ pint milk	1 tbsp olive oil
1 oz butter	1 large tomato
4 oz grated cheese	1 tsp cornflour
salt and pepper	flour

Proceed as for above recipe using only 2 oz of the grated cheese. When the dumplings are cooked put them in an ovenproof dish and cover with a sauce made by heating the olive oil and stirring in the cornflour and well-crushed tomato. Sprinkle with the remaining 2 oz of grated cheese and bake 10 minutes in a hot oven.

POMMES DE TERRE A LA BASQUE

Ingredients

8 medium-sized potatoes	pepper
2 oz flour	1 tbsp chopped parsley
2 oz butter	2 shallots
½ pint milk	2 anchovy fillets
	2 eggs

Hard boil the eggs. Peel the potatoes, cut in halves and scoop out centres to form into barques. Boil 5 minutes in a pan of salted water. Drain and put side by side in a large ovenproof dish. Make a sauce by melting the butter, stirring in the flour and adding, gradually, the milk. Stir until it thickens. Chop together the shallots and anchovy fillets and add the parsley, pepper and crushed eggs. Blend in the sauce. Fill the potato barques with this mixture. Add to the dish half a pint of water and the butter. Bake 40 minutes in a moderate oven.

PALETS
(fried potato cakes)

Ingredients

1 lb potatoes	1 egg
2 oz olive oil	½ cup chopped chives
1 oz flour	salt and pepper

Peel the potatoes and grate. Put in a bowl and add the well-beaten eggs, seasoning, flour and chives. Heat the olive oil in a frying-pan and on it place, without touching each other, spoonfuls of the raw potato mixture. Flatten and fry on each side until golden. Add more salt on serving.

13

ROOT VEGETABLES

Beetroot, Celery, Celeriac, Jerusalem Artichokes, Salsifis, Turnips and Parsnips

Of all root vegetables, beetroot is mostly associated with salads. Yet it is also delicious when served hot, often with a parsley sauce, and the very young, small beetroot need only an hour or so's cooking. It is also good with sour cream, well seasoned with paprika.

The beetroot is a native of the more temperate parts of the world, where its fleshy roots have for long been a valuable food for man and domestic animals as well as a source of sugar.

In fact, it is the slightly sweet flavour which makes it popular with children. Its sugar content is energy giving as well as containing mineral salts and vitamins. It makes a refreshing hors d'oeuvre and is very digestible.

Always cooked in their skins, they can be either boiled or baked, but in either case need long, slow cooking. They should always be firm and never slimy to the touch.

Radishes, too, are usually associated with salads, although in France they are usually served as an hors d'oeuvre on their own. *Radis – beurre,* a term often seen on restaurant menus, means simply radishes with bread and butter.

There are six varieties which include long-rooted and spindle-shaped, round and turnip-rooted.

The *radis noir*, or horseradish, is to be found principally in the Jewish quarters in France. It is considered particularly efficacious in relieving complaints of the gall bladder.

The origin of the garden radish is doubtful, but we know that it was grown at an early period in Egypt and that it has for long been cultivated in India and China. It was introduced into Britain over three centuries ago.

For winter salads celeriac is excellent, known as *céleri rémoulade* when served with mayonnaise.

The use of the stalks of celery to accompany hard cheese is now becoming popular in France. For this, the green outer stalks, which are often hollow, should be discarded. While celery is not a root crop, it is convenient to consider it here. Its particularly delicate flavour makes it a valuable addition to soups, sauces and salads.

Celery juice is diuretic. It also has a curious medical value as a cure for chilblains, by soaking for ten minutes the affected parts in a bath in which half a pound of celery has been boiled in two pints of water for forty-five minutes.

Jerusalem artichokes are again returning to favour. Their unpopularity was probably largely due to their nobbly surface which made them difficult to peel. Those being cultivated now, however, are much smoother, thus facilitating their preparation. It is easiest to parboil them before peeling, although their slightly nutty flavour makes them also good raw, grated as celeriac.

They belong to the same family as the sunflower. The prefix of 'Jerusalem' is a corruption of the Italian *girasole* (sunflower), while 'artichoke' implies a resemblance in flavour to globe artichokes. They originated in America and are rich in glucose.

Salsify is often shunned probably for the same reason as the globe artichoke, the tiresome business of scraping the black skin. A native of northern Europe and Siberia, it has for long been cultivated on account of the delicate flavour of its roots. The young stalks are delicious in salads while the flowers give a distinctive flavour to omelettes. Once scraped, they should be put immediately into cold water as they discolour very quickly.

The cultivation of turnips dates back to the time of the ancient Greeks and Romans when they were esteemed as next in utility to cereals. There is no record of their introduction into England but it is known that during the reign of Henry VIII they used to be baked or roasted in ashes and that they were a basic food before potatoes were known.

Nowadays they tend to be considered more as an addition

to stews than as a vegetable in their own right, although in fact there are a number of delicious ways of serving them, while the tender tops can be used for salads.

Parsnips, too, are now used chiefly in stews and soups, although they can also be prepared in the same way as turnips. They have for long been cultivated in Europe and Western Asia and in the times of the ancient Romans were particularly favoured as an accompaniment to dried fish.

SALADE DE BETTERAVES (1)
(beetroot salad)

Ingredients	
4 small beetroot	3 tbsp olive oil
¼ cup grated horseradish	1 tbsp wine vinegar
salt	1 shallot
	cupful chopped parsley

Scrub well the beetroot and boil until tender. Peel and slice. When cold, mix thoroughly with the horseradish, salt, oil and vinegar. Sprinkle with the parsley and chopped shallot.

SALADE DE BETTERAVES (2)

Ingredients	
2 large cooked beetroot	yolk of an egg
2 slightly tart dessert	tsp vinegar
apples	pinch of mustard powder
juice of half a lemon	olive oil
1 tbsp sultanas	salt and pepper

Slice the cold beetroot and dress with mayonnaise made as follows. Put the egg yolk in a bowl with the mustard powder and beat. Add the oil, drop by drop, beating all the time until a creamy consistency is obtained. Add the vinegar and seasoning.

BETTERAVES FARCIES (1)
(stuffed beetroot)

Ingredients
2 medium-sized beetroot
2 tbsp cooked peas
2 tbsp chopped cooked
  carrots
yolk of an egg
tsp lemon juice
pinch of mustard powder
olive oil
salt and pepper

Scrub well the beetroot and boil until tender. Drain and peel. Cut in halves and scoop out the centres. Chop these finely and add the peas and carrots. Mix well with a mayonnaise made as in the previous recipe but replacing the vinegar by the lemon juice. Fill the beetroot halves with this mixture.

BETTERAVES FARCIES (2)

Ingredients
2 medium-sized beetroot
cupful boiled rice
½ cup finely chopped mint
salt and pepper
3 tbsp olive oil
1 tbsp vinegar

Prepare the beetroot as above and cut in halves. Scoop out the centres, chop finely and add to the rice and mint. Mix well with the oil, vinegar and seasoning. Fill beetroot halves.

BETTERAVES A LA BÉCHAMEL

Ingredients
1 lb small beetroot
2 oz butter
1 oz flour
½ pint milk
salt and pepper

Scrub well the beetroot, boil until tender and peel. Serve with a *béchamel* sauce made by melting the butter, stirring in the flour and then, gradually, adding the milk. Stir until it thickens and season.

BETTERAVES A LA CRÈME

Ingredients
1 lb small beetroot
½ pint hot water
yolk of an egg
2 oz butter
1 oz flour
2 oz cream

Prepare the beetroot as in previous recipe and serve with a sauce made by melting the butter, stirring in the flour and then, gradually, the hot water. Stir until it thickens. Off the heat add the beaten egg yolk and blend in the cream.

BETTERAVES A LA BOURGUIGNONNE

Ingredients
1 lb beetroot
1 tbsp olive oil
2 bacon rashers
12 small onions

1 tsp flour
½ pint red wine
croûtons (small squares of stale bread fried in butter)

Prepare the beetroot, peel and dice. Chop the bacon small and fry lightly in the oil together with the onions. Add the flour, wine, seasoning and beetroot. Bring to the boil and simmer 10 minutes. Top with the *croûtons* on serving.

BETTERAVES AU FOUR
(beetroot in the oven)

Ingredients
2 medium-sized beetroot
2 tbsp white wine
2 oz fine breadcrumbs
salt and pepper

½ cup chopped parsley and sage
1 oz butter
1 oz grated Parmesan cheese

Prepare the beetroot, cut in halves and scoop out the centres. Dice these and fry gently in the butter together with the crumbs for 2 minutes. Add seasoning, wine, parsley and sage and simmer a further minute. Fill the beetroot halves with this mixture and top with the Parmesan. Put in an ovenproof dish of which the bottom has been covered with olive oil. Bake in a moderate oven for 15 minutes.

BETTERAVES FRITES
(fried beetroot)

Ingredients
2 medium-sized beetroot
1 onion
2 garlic cloves

1 tbsp chopped parsley
2 oz olive oil
juice of half a lemon

Boil the beetroot, peel and dice. Heat the oil and gently fry the beetroot with the chopped onion and garlic for 10 minutes. Season and add the lemon juice and parsley on serving.

BETTERAVES RAPÉES
(grated beetroot)

Ingredients	
2 medium-sized beetroot	2 garlic cloves
2 oz butter	1 tsp vinegar
1 onion	1 tbsp grated orange rind
	seasoning

Scrub well the beetroot, peel and grate. Melt the butter and dry the raw, grated beetroot together with the chopped onion, garlic and orange rind for 10 minutes. Add the vinegar and seasoning and serve.

CÉLERI A LA MAÎTRE D'HÔTEL

Ingredients	
½ lb celery	2 oz butter
½ pint meat stock	½ cup chopped parsley

Wash well the celery, removing the green hollow outer stalks. Cut into lengths of about 2 inches and boil in salted water for 10 minutes. Drain and finish cooking in the stock. Melt the butter, add the celery, parsley and a little of the stock and turn for 2 minutes.

CÉLERI AU JUS

Ingredients	
1 lb celery	tbsp cooking juices from a
½ pint meat stock	roast

Prepare and cook the celery as in above recipe. Drain and return to pan with the meat juices.

CÉLERI VILLAGEOISE

Ingredients
¼ lb celery   1 tsp vinegar
1 tsp mustard powder   2 oz cream

Prepare the celery and cut into very thin strips. Mix the mustard powder with the vinegar and add to the cream. Mix well with the celery and refrigerate.

CÉLERI AU GRATIN
(celery with cheese)

Ingredients
¼ lb celery   1 oz flour
2 oz butter   salt and pepper
¼ pint meat stock   2 oz grated cheese

Prepare the celery as above and boil 20 minutes. Drain. Melt the butter, stir in the flour and add, gradually, the meat stock and seasoning. Put the celery in a buttered oven-proof dish. Cover with the sauce and top with the cheese. Bake in a hot oven until golden.

CÉLERI A LA BÉCHAMEL

Ingredients   1 oz flour
¼ lb celery   ¼ pint milk
2 oz butter   seasoning

Prepare the celery and boil in salted water until tender. Drain and dress with a *béchamel* sauce made by melting the butter, stirring in the flour and adding, gradually, the milk and seasoning. Stir until it thickens.

CÉLERI AU FROMAGE
(celery in a cheese sauce)

Ingredients
¼ lb celery   2 oz grated cheese
3 oz butter   ¼ pint milk
1 oz flour   salt and pepper

Prepare and cook the celery as in above recipe. Stir the grated cheese into the sauce. Put celery into a well-buttered ovenproof dish. Cover with the sauce and dot with the remaining ounce of butter. Bake 5 minutes in a hot oven.

CÉLERI EN BEIGNETS
(celery fritters)

Ingredients
4 celery stalks
1 egg

1 pint milk
3 tbsp flour
salt and pepper

Prepare the celery, cutting into lengths of about 2 inches. Cook and drain. Prepare a batter by putting the flour in a bowl and making a well in the centre. Into this break the egg and then add, gradually, the milk. Blend well and add seasoning. Cover and stand 2 hours. Dip the celery pieces into this and fry in deep fat.

CÉLERI RÉMOULADE
(celeriac in mayonnaise)

Ingredients
1 celeriac
1 tsp mustard powder
1 tbsp vinegar

olive oil
1 egg yolk
salt and pepper

Wash and peel the celeriac. Grate and mix well with a mayonnaise made by putting the egg yolk into a bowl together with the mustard powder and beating well. Then add the oil, drop by drop, beating until a creamy consistency is obtained. Add the vinegar and seasoning.

CÉLERI-RAVE FRIT
(fried celeriac)

Ingredients
1 celeriac
2 oz butter

salt and pepper
½ cup chopped parsley

Wash and peel the celeriac. Cut into cubes and fry in the butter and seasoning. Sprinkle with the parsley on serving.

CÉLERI-RAVE EN PURÉE

Ingredients
1 celeriac
2 tbsp of juices from a
  roast

salt and pepper
croûtons (small squares of
  stale bread fried in
  butter)

Wash and peel the celeriac. Chop small and boil in salted water until tender. Force through vegetable mill and return to pan with the seasoning and meat juices. Simmer 2 minutes and serve with the *croûtons*.

CÉLERI-RAVE FARCI
(stuffed celeriac)

Ingredients
2 small celeriacs
¼ lb mushrooms
2 shallots

2 oz butter
tsp flour
½ pint milk
salt and pepper

Wash and peel the celeriacs. Cut in halves. Boil 20 minutes and drain. Lightly fry the sliced mushrooms and shallots in 1 oz of the butter, stir in the flour and add the milk and seasoning. Mix with the scooped-out centres of the celeriacs. Put in a well-buttered ovenproof dish. Dot with the remaining butter and bake 40 minutes in a slow oven.

CÉLERI-RAVE AU MADÈRE
(celeriac in Madeira wine)

Ingredients
1 celeriac
2 oz Madeira wine

meat stock
white wine
salt and pepper

Prepare the celeriac, cut into cubes and put in a pan. Cover with part white wine and part meat stock. Season, bring to the boil and simmer until tender. Remove the celeriac and keep warm. Boil fast the liquid until only about a tbsp remains. Add the Madeira wine and pour over the celeriac.

CÉLERI-RAVE A LA NIÇOISE

Ingredients

1 celeriac	2 mushrooms
2 oz butter	salt and pepper
1 large ripe tomato	2 oz grated cheese
2 garlic cloves	1 oz olive oil

Wash and peel the celeriac and cut into pieces the size of potato chips. Boil in salted water. When part cooked drain and finish cooking in the butter. In the olive oil lightly fry the chopped mushrooms and garlic. Stir in the crushed tomato and seasoning and simmer a further 2 minutes. Put this sauce in an ovenproof dish, add the celeriac and top with the grated cheese. Brown in a hot oven.

CÉLERI-RAVE BRAISÉ

Ingredients

1 celeriac	½ pint meat stock
2 oz butter	1 oz flour
	salt and pepper

Prepare the celeriac and boil 10 minutes. Melt the butter, stir in the flour and add, gradually, the stock and seasoning. Simmer the celeriac in this for 20 minutes.

CÉLERI-RAVE SOUBISE
(celeriac in onion sauce)

Ingredients

1 celeriac	3 oz butter
¼ lb onions	1 oz grated Parmesan
1 oz flour	cheese
	salt and pepper

Prepare the celeriac, chop into cubes and boil 30 minutes. Drain, reserving the cooking water. Melt 2 oz of the butter and lightly fry the sliced onions. Stir in the flour and add, gradually, a quarter of a pint of the cooking water and seasoning. Stir until it thickens. Put the celeriac in an ovenproof dish. Cover with the sauce and top with the Parmesan cheese. Dot with the remaining butter.

TOPINAMBOURS A LA MAÎTRE D'HÔTEL

Ingredients

1 lb Jerusalem artichokes	½ cup chopped parsley
2 oz butter	salt and pepper

Wash and peel the artichokes and boil until tender (about 30 minutes). Drain and return to pan with the butter, parsley and seasoning. Turn for 2 minutes.

TOPINAMBOURS AU JUS

Ingredients	salt and pepper
1 lb Jerusalem artichokes	2 tbsp juices from a roast

Prepare and cook the artichokes as above. Drain and return to pan with the meat juices for a further 2 minutes.

TOPINAMBOURS A LA CRÈME

Ingredients	½ cup chopped tarragon
1 lb Jerusalem artichokes	salt and pepper
3 oz butter	juice of half a lemon

Wash and peel the artichokes. Slice and fry gently in the butter until tender. Add seasoning and lemon juice. Off the heat blend in the cream and sprinkle with the tarragon on serving.

TOPINAMBOURS FRITS

Ingredients

½ lb Jerusalem artichokes	½ pint milk
1 egg	salt and pepper
3 tbsp flour	¼ cup chopped parsley

Wash and peel the artichokes. Cut into slices and drain. Prepare a batter by putting the flour in a bowl with a well in the centre. Into this break the egg and stir in, gradually, the milk. Add seasoning, cover and stand for 2 hours. Dip the artichoke slices in this batter and fry in deep fat. Sprinkle with the parsley on serving.

PURÉE DE TOPINAMBOURS

Ingredients

1 lb Jerusalem artichokes	2 oz butter
pinch of grated nutmeg	½ pint milk
salt and pepper	1 oz flour

Prepare the artichokes, chop small and boil until tender. Force through vegetable mill and return to pan with a *béchamel* sauce made by melting the butter, stirring in the flour and adding, gradually, the milk and seasoning. Stir for 2 minutes.

TOPINAMBOURS A LA PROVENÇAL

Ingredients

1 lb Jerusalem artichokes	salt
meat stock	pinch of grated nutmeg
pinch of Cayenne pepper	2 garlic cloves
tsp of ginger	½ cup chopped parsley

Wash and peel the artichokes. Slice and place in pan with the Cayenne, salt, ginger and nutmeg. Add sufficient stock to cover and boil until the liquid is nearly absorbed. Mix the chopped garlic with the parsley and add to the artichokes on serving.

TOPINAMBOURS AUX FINES HERBES
(Jerusalem artichokes with herbs)

Ingredients

1 lb Jerusalem artichokes	cupful mixed herbs as
2 ripe tomatoes	available
3 oz olive oil	salt and pepper

Prepare the artichokes and slice. Fry gently in the olive oil. When nearly cooked add the crushed tomato, herbs and seasoning. Continue cooking until tender.

TOPINAMBOURS EN SALADE
(salad of Jerusalem artichokes)

Ingredients
1 lb Jerusalem artichokes
1 celery stalk
2 oz olive oil
juice of half a lemon
¼ cup chopped parsley

Prepare the artichokes and boil until just tender. Slice and while still hot mix with the oil, lemon juice, seasoning and chopped celery. Refrigerate and sprinkle with the parsley on serving.

SALSIFIS A LA MAÎTRE D'HÔTEL

Ingredients
1 lb salsify
2 oz butter
¼ cup chopped parsley
seasoning

Scrub and thoroughly scrape the salsify, plunging at once into cold water. Boil until tender (about 45 minutes). Drain and return to pan with the butter and parsley. Turn well for 2 minutes.

SALSIFIS AU JUS

Ingredients
1 lb salsify
salt and pepper
2 tbsp juices from a roast

Prepare and cook the salsify as in above recipe. Drain and return to pan with the meat juices for a further 2 minutes.

SALSIFIS A LA CRÈME

Ingredients
1 lb salsify
2 oz butter
1 oz flour
1 oz cream
1 shallot
salt and pepper

Prepare and cook the salsify. Drain and put in a vegetable dish. Cover with a sauce made by melting the butter and stirring in the flour, well chopped shallot and seasoning. Blend in the cream.

SALSIFIS A LA POULETTE

Ingredients
1 lb salsify
2 oz butter

salt and pepper
1 tbsp chopped parsley
1 egg

Prepare and cook the salsify. Drain and put in vegetable dish. Cover with a sauce made by melting the butter, stirring in the flour and 2 tbsp of water. Add the parsley. Off the heat blend in the well-beaten egg.

SALSIFIS AU FROMAGE
(salsify with a cheese sauce)

Ingredients
1 lb salsify
2 oz butter
1 oz flour
½ pint milk

2 oz grated cheese
cupful browned bread-
    crumbs
salt and pepper

Prepare and cook the salsify. Drain and put in an ovenproof dish. Melt the butter, stir in the flour and add, gradually, the milk. Stir until it thickens. Add the seasoning and grated cheese. Cover the salsify with this sauce and top with the breadcrumbs. Bake 15 minutes in a moderate oven.

BEIGNETS AU SALSIFIS
(salsify fritters)

Ingredients
8 small salsify
1 lemon
1 egg

4 oz flour
¼ pint milk
salt and pepper

First make the batter by putting the flour and seasoning into a bowl, making a well in the centre. Into this break the egg. Beat well and add the milk gradually. Cover and leave in a warm place for 2 hours. Prepare and cook the salsify. Drain. Dip in the batter mixture and fry in deep fat. Serve with the lemon juice.

SALSIFIS A LA PROVENÇALE

Ingredients
1 lb salsify
¼ lb ripe tomatoes

3 garlic cloves
1 oz olive oil
salt and pepper

Prepare and cook the salsify. Drain. Heat the olive oil, add the crushed tomato and chopped garlic. Fry lightly for 5 minutes. Add the salsify and continue cooking a further 5 minutes.

SALSIFIS EN SALADE

(salad of salsify)

Ingredients
1 lb salsify, including the flowers and the tender part of the stalks

1 shallot
2 tbsp olive oil
juice of half a lemon
salt and pepper

Prepare the salsify, setting aside the flowers and the stalks. Boil the roots until tender and drain. When cold put in salad bowl with the well-chopped stalks and flowers. Mix well with the olive oil, lemon juice and seasoning.

SALSIFY A LA NORMANDE

Ingredients
1 lb salsify
2 oz butter
2 shallots
1 tsp flour

½ pint cider
pinch of grated nutmeg
1 tsp lemon juice
2 oz cream

Prepare and cook the salsify. Drain and keep warm. Melt the butter and in it fry the sliced shallots until yellow. Stir in the flour and, a little at a time, the cider. Add the seasoning, nutmeg and lemon juice and blend in the cream. Pour this sauce over the salsify.

NAVETS AU JUS

Ingredients
1 lb turnips
2 oz butter
salt and pepper

2 tbsp juices from
   a roast
½ pint meat stock
bouquet garni

Scrub, peel and slice the turnips. Melt the butter and add the turnips. Fry lightly until golden. Add the meat juices, stock, seasoning and *bouquet garni*. Bring to the boil and simmer 1 hour or until tender. Remove *bouquet garni* before serving.

NAVETS A LA BÉCHAMEL

Ingredients	
1 lb turnips	2 oz butter
½ pint milk	1 oz flour
	salt and pepper

Prepare the turnips, cut into slices and boil until tender. Drain, put in a vegetable dish and cover with a sauce made by melting the butter, stirring in the flour and adding, gradually, the milk. Stir until it thickens and add seasoning.

NAVETS A LA POULETTE

Ingredients	
1 lb turnips	salt and pepper
2 oz butter	1 tbsp chopped parsley
2 tbsp water	1 egg

Prepare and slice the turnips. Cook until tender. Drain. Put in vegetable dish and cover with a sauce made by melting the butter, stirring in the flour, water and parsley; then, off the heat, blend in the well-beaten egg.

NAVETS GLACÉS
(glazed turnips)

Ingredients	
1 lb young turnips	1 tbsp sugar
2 oz butter	2 tbsp juices from a roast

Prepare the turnips, slice, and boil 10 minutes. Drain and cook gently in the butter for 20 minutes. Add sugar and meat juices and simmer for 1 hour, adding a little liquid if necessary.

NAVETS AUX FINES HERBES

(turnips with herbs)

Ingredients
1 lb turnips
cupful mixed herbs as
  available

1 shallot
1 cup browned bread-
  crumbs
salt and pepper

Prepare the turnips, slice and boil for 10 minutes. Drain. Melt the butter and add the chopped shallot, herbs and turnips. Cook gently until tender. Stir in the breadcrumbs and cook a further few minutes.

NAVETS FARCIS

(stuffed turnips)

Ingredients
2 medium-sized turnips
2 oz butter

$\frac{1}{4}$ lb mushrooms
salt and pepper

Prepare the turnips and boil for 20 minutes. Drain, cut in halves and scoop out the centres. Wash these. Lightly fry the mushrooms and add, together with the seasoning. Return to shells and put in a buttered ovenproof dish. Cover and bake in a moderate oven for 45 minutes.

NAVETS AU CIDRE

(turnips in cider)

Ingredients
2 medium-sized turnips
1 egg
$\frac{1}{4}$ pint cider

1 shallot
2 tbsp juices from a roast
bouquet garni
salt and pepper

Prepare the turnips and boil for 20 minutes. Drain and cut in halves. Scoop out the centres and mash together with the chopped shallot, seasoning and well-beaten egg. Put in an ovenproof dish with the cider, meat juices and *bouquet garni*. Cover and bake 45 minutes in a moderate oven. Remove *bouquet garni* before serving.

NAVETS PROVENÇALE

(fried turnips)

Ingredients

1 lb young turnips	1 tsp sugar
2 oz olive oil	2 tbsp tomato *coulis*
2 cloves garlic	(see page 188)
1 cup chopped parsley	salt and pepper

Prepare the turnips and boil 10 minutes. Drain and fry in the olive oil together with the chopped garlic, until tender. Add sugar, seasoning, parsley and tomato *coulis* and cook a further 5 minutes.

PANAIS A LA SAUCE

(parsnips in herb sauce)

Ingredients

1 lb parsnips	2 cloves
½ cup chopped parsley	dsp chopped basil
2 oz butter	1 tsp flour
tbsp chopped chives	2 egg yolks
2 chopped garlic cloves	1 tsp wine vinegar
2 chopped shallots	2 tbsp meat stock
	salt and pepper

Scrub and peel the parsnips and boil for 3 minutes. Slice and cook gently in the butter together with the parsley, chives, shallots, garlic, cloves, basil and seasoning for 5 minutes. Add the flour and meat stock and simmer a further 2 minutes. Add the well-beaten egg yolks and the vinegar and serve immediately.

PANAIS RÔTIS

(roast parsnips)

Ingredients

½ lb parsnips	salt and pepper
1 tbsp sugar	1 oz butter

Prepare the parsnips and boil 20 minutes. Drain, slice and put in an ovenproof dish with the butter and seasoning. Sprinkle with the sugar and bake in a moderate oven for 20 minutes.

14

SPINACH AND OTHER LEAF VEGETABLES

Sorrel, Dandelion, Chard, Chicory and Lettuce

The usual treatment of leaf vegetables is to boil them, but both sorrel and chicory also make good salads. On the other hand lettuce, generally considered as a salad, can well be served as a vegetable should there be a glut, as well as making good soup.

Chicory is often called Belgian endive, since it was there that it originated. The roots, when roasted, are used as a substitute for coffee and, in the opinion of many, improve the flavour when mixed with coffee.

By boiling for a few minutes, draining and then putting into fresh water chicory tastes less bitter. But in fact it has a better flavour as well as being more nourishing when simply steamed or boiled in a minimum of water with the addition of a little butter. It can also be cooked in the oven.

To prepare, the base should be removed by slicing off with a sharp knife and any wilted outer leaves discarded.

Spinach, which originated in Siberia, passed westwards to reach Britain three centuries ago.

It yields from April until November and on account of its rapid growth needs constant picking to prevent it from running to seed. It needs a rich soil, however, to bring out its best flavour.

It needs careful washing and should be cooked in a minimum of water. There are a number of interesting ways of serving it other than just plain boiled as an accompaniment to meat.

It also makes a useful green colouring. For this, having first washed the spinach and discarded the stems, the leaves should be packed as closely as possible in a pan with a tablespoon only of water and reduced to a pulp over a very low heat. It should then be put into a cloth to squeeze out any liquid still remaining and stored in screw-topped jars. It can be kept thus in the refrigerator for up to three months.

Sorrel, as well as being used in salads and soups, can also be served in the same way as spinach but on account of its slightly bitter flavour is best used in small quantities.

Also slightly bitter, the dandelion, although one of the most objectionable of weeds, is a gourmet treat in many parts of the world. Nettles were often used as a vegetable in the past but were never grown commercially as are dandelions today in France. They can be prepared, as well as a salad, in much the same way as spinach.

Cardons or *blettes*, known as Swiss chard, are sometimes to be found in English shops. The large fleshy leaves can be prepared as celery stalks or cooked chicory, discarding the outer leaves. In order to keep white it should be put, after washing, into water with the addition of lemon juice for a few minutes.

ÉPINARDS AU JUS

Ingredients
1½ lb spinach   2 tbsp of the juices from a
salt and pepper   roast

Thoroughly wash the spinach, removing the thick part of the stalks. Boil with the addition of a cupful of water until tender. Drain well and return to pan with the seasoning and meat juices.

ÉPINARDS AU BEURRE

Ingredients   salt and pepper
1½ lb spinach   2 oz butter

Prepare and cook the spinach as in above recipe. Drain and return to pan with the butter and seasoning. Heat through.

ÉPINARDS A LA CRÈME

Ingredients
1¼ lb spinach
2 oz butter

salt and pepper
pinch of grated nutmeg
2 oz cream

Prepare and cook the spinach as above. Drain and return to pan with the butter, seasoning and nutmeg. Heat the cream and blend in, simmering for a further 2 minutes.

PURÉE D'ÉPINARDS

Ingredients
1¼ lb spinach
3 oz butter

¼ pint milk
salt and pepper

Prepare and cook the spinach as above. Drain, sieve and stir in the butter, milk and seasoning. Return to pan to heat through, turning well.

ÉPINARDS A LA BÉCHAMEL

Ingredients
1¼ lb spinach
2 oz butter

1 oz flour
½ pint milk
salt and pepper

Prepare the spinach and boil for 5 minutes. Drain and chop. Melt the butter, stir in the flour and add, gradually, the milk. Blend in the spinach and seasoning and simmer a further 5 minutes, stirring frequently.

ÉPINARDS EN BOUILLABAISSE

Ingredients
1¼ lb spinach
1 tbsp olive oil
2 shallots
3 medium-sized potatoes
2 garlic cloves

4 eggs
½ tsp saffron
salt
croûtons (small squares of
    stale bread fried in
    butter)

Prepare and boil the spinach. Drain. In the oil lightly fry the chopped shallots and garlic. Add the peeled and sliced potatoes and cook until the potatoes are soft. Add the spinach, saffron and salt and over this pour ¼ pint of boiling water. Simmer for half an hour. Break in the eggs and poach until set. Serve accompanied by the *croûtons*.

ÉPINARDS AU GRATIN
(baked spinach)

Ingredients	
1½ lb spinach	1 cup browned bread- crumbs
2 eggs	1 shallot
1 oz butter	½ cup chopped parsley

Prepare and boil the spinach. Drain, saving the liquid, and put the spinach in a well-buttered ovenproof dish. Beat the eggs with the liquid, add the parsley and finely chopped shallots and pour over the spinach. Cover with the breadcrumbs and bake 10 minutes in a moderate oven.

ÉPINARDS AU FROMAGE
(spinach with cheese sauce)

Ingredients	
1½ lb spinach	½ pint milk
2 oz butter	salt
1 oz flour	pinch of Cayenne pepper
	2 oz Parmesan cheese

Prepare and boil the spinach. Drain and put in a well-buttered ovenproof dish. Melt the butter, stir in the flour and add, gradually, the milk. Stir until it thickens. Add seasoning, and pour this sauce over the spinach. Top with the Parmesan and bake 20 minutes in a hot oven.

SOUFFLÉ D'ÉPINARDS

Ingredients	
1 lb spinach	1 oz flour
3 eggs	½ pint milk
2 oz butter	pinch of nutmeg
	salt and pepper

Prepare and boil the spinach. Drain. Melt the butter, stir in the flour and add, gradually, the milk. Stir until it thickens. Add salt, pepper, and nutmeg. Cool slightly and blend in the egg yolks. Mix well with the spinach. Whip the whites until stiff and add. Put in a well-buttered soufflé dish and bake 25 minutes in a hot oven, or until well risen.

ÉPINARDS A LA PROVENÇALE

Ingredients

1½ lb spinach
1 tbsp olive oil
3 garlic cloves
2 tbsp slivered almonds
salt and pepper

1 tbsp chopped green
  olives
1 tbsp chopped black
  olives
1 tbsp capers

Prepare the spinach and boil 5 minutes. Drain and chop. Heat the oil and in it fry gently the chopped garlic and almonds; add the olives, capers, seasoning and spinach, and re-heat.

ÉPINARDS EN GELÉE

(spinach in aspic)

Ingredients

1 lb spinach
¼ lb mushrooms
½ pint milk
3 eggs

1 oz powdered gelatine
pinch of nutmeg
pinch of mustard powder
salt and pepper

Scrub and slice the mushrooms and cover in olive oil. Stand for 2 hours, turning occasionally. Wash and chop the spinach. Scald the milk and pour over two of the well-beaten eggs. Add seasoning and nutmeg. Stir in the un-cooked spinach. Dissolve the gelatine in a little hot water and add. Pour into a greased ring. Set ring in a pan of water and bake 30 minutes. Turn out when cold. Fill centre with the mushrooms well mixed with a mayonnaise made as follows: put egg yolk in a bowl with the mustard powder and beat; add the oil, drop by drop, beating all the time until a creamy consistency is obtained; add the vinegar and seasoning.

ÉPINARDS EN CRÊPES

(spinach pancakes)

Ingredients

3 tbsp self-raising flour	salt and pepper
½ pint milk	2 oz grated cheese
1 egg	butter as required

First make the batter by putting the flour in a bowl and making a well in the centre. Into this break the egg and beat well. Stir in the milk and seasoning. Cover and stand for 2 hours. Prepare and boil the spinach. Drain and chop. Make the pancakes in the usual way. Fill each with spinach, roll up and put side by side in an ovenproof dish. Sprinkle with the grated cheese and dot with pieces of butter. Bake 10 minutes in a hot oven.

OMELETTE AUX ÉPINARDS

Ingredients

½ lb spinach	salt and pepper
1 oz olive oil	4 eggs
	2 oz butter

Wash and chop the spinach and boil 2 minutes. Drain and put in a pan with the butter over a gentle heat until the spinach softens. Break eggs into a bowl and beat. Add spinach and seasoning. Heat the oil in omelette pan and pour in the egg and spinach mixture. Finish in the usual way, serving either hot or cold.

CROQUETTES D'ÉPINARDS

(spinach balls)

Ingredients

1 lb spinach	3 oz butter
½ lb potatoes	½ pint milk
	salt and pepper

Peel and boil the potatoes until tender. Force through vegetable mill, and blend in ¼ pint milk and 1 oz butter. Boil the spinach, sieve and stir in the remaining 2 oz of butter and ¼ pint of milk. Mix well with the potato purée.

Form into balls, flattening top and bottom. Roll in flour and fry in a mixture of olive oil and butter until golden on both sides.

ÉPINARDS EN SALADE (1)

Ingredients

¼ lb spinach	1 tsp vinegar
4 bacon rashers	1 tsp lemon juice
3 oz olive oil	salt and pepper

Wash and drain the spinach. Fry the bacon until very crisp. Crumble and mix with the chopped raw spinach. In salad bowl mix the seasoning with the vinegar and lemon juice. Blend in the oil and add the spinach and bacon. Toss well half an hour before serving.

ÉPINARDS EN SALADE (2)

Ingredients

1¼ lb spinach	juice of half a lemon
2 oz cream	salt and pepper
	2 eggs

Hard boil the eggs and shell. Prepare and boil the spinach. Drain, pressing down so that absolutely no liquid remains. Combine the cream, lemon juice and seasoning. When cold, add the chopped spinach and sprinkle with the minced eggs.

ÉPINARDS EN SUBRICS
(spinach garniture)

Ingredients

1¼ lb spinach	pinch of grated nutmeg
2 eggs	1 oz butter
2 oz olive oil	salt and pepper

Prepare and boil the spinach. Drain. Melt the butter and add the spinach. Stir for 2 minutes. Add the well-beaten eggs, nutmeg and seasoning. Mix well. In a frying-pan heat the olive oil and put in dessertspoons of the spinach, taking care that they do not touch. When firm turn and fry on the other sides. Serve round a roast of meat.

TARTE D'ÉPINARDS

Ingredients
1 lb spinach
short pastry (2 oz butter
   to 5 oz flour)
2 oz cream

1 oz butter
2 oz grated Gruyère
   cheese
2 oz Parmesan cheese
pinch of Cayenne pepper

Bake the pastry blind in an 8-inch flan tin. Prepare and boil the spinach. Sieve and mix with the butter, cream, Gruyère cheese and Cayenne pepper. Cover flan with this mixture and top with the Parmesan cheese. Bake in a hot oven until the cheese is golden.

OSEILLE AU JUS

Ingredients
1 lb sorrel

salt and pepper
2 tbsp juices from a roast

Thoroughly wash the sorrel, removing the hard stems of the larger leaves, and boil in a minimum of salted water. Drain and return to pan with the seasoning and meat juices for 2 minutes.

PURÉE D'OSEILLE

Ingredients
1 lb sorrel
yolk of an egg

¼ pint milk
1 oz butter
salt and pepper

Prepare the sorrel and boil for 10 minutes. Drain and sieve. Stir in the butter, milk, egg yolk and seasoning. Return to pan and heat through.

OSEILLE AU BLANC

Ingredients

1 lb sorrel	salt and pepper
½ pint meat stock	tsp sugar
2 oz butter	3 egg yolks
1 oz flour	1 oz cream

Wash the sorrel, boil 5 minutes and drain. Melt 1 oz of the butter, stir in the flour and add the sorrel, seasoning and meat stock. Simmer 30 minutes and sieve. Return to pan with the remaining ounce of butter, the cream and the well-beaten egg yolks. Heat through.

CRÈME D'OSEILLE

Ingredients

1 lb sorrel	2 tbsp cream
2 oz butter	salt and pepper

Prepare the sorrel and cook in the butter until soft. Stir in the cream and seasoning and heat through.

OSEILLE EN OMELETTE

Ingredients

½ lb sorrel	4 eggs
tsp of sugar	salt and pepper
	2 oz butter

Prepare the sorrel and cook gently in butter until soft. Add sugar and seasoning. Make omelette (or omelettes) in the usual way, filling with the sorrel.

CARDONS AU JUS

Ingredients

1 lb chards	2 tbsp juices from a roast
1 dsp arrowroot	salt and pepper

Wash the chards, discarding the outer leaves and cut into lengths of about 2 inches. Boil in salted water, with the addition of a dessertspoon of vinegar, until tender. Drain and return to pan with the arrowroot, meat juices and seasoning. Simmer a further 2 minutes.

CARDONS AU GRATIN
(baked chards)

Ingredients
1 lb chards
¼ lb mushrooms
salt and pepper

juice of half a lemon
2 oz butter
cupful browned bread-
    crumbs

Prepare the chards and boil until tender. Drain. In a separate pan boil the mushrooms and mince with a cupful of the chard, the lemon juice and seasoning. Cover the bottom of a buttered ovenproof dish with half of this mixture. Add the remainder of the chards and cover with the rest of the mushroom mixture. Melt the butter and add. Top with the breadcrumbs and bake 20 minutes in a moderate oven.

CARDONS AU PARMESAN

Ingredients
1 lb chards
2 oz Parmesan cheese
2 oz butter

1 oz flour
½ pint milk
salt and pepper

Prepare and boil the chards. Drain and put in an ovenproof dish. Make a sauce by melting the butter, stirring in the flour and adding, gradually, the milk. Season and pour over the chards. Top with the Parmesan cheese and bake 20 minutes in a moderate oven.

ENDIVES A L'ÉTUVÉE
(steamed chicory)

Ingredients
8 chicory heads
2 oz butter

juice of a lemon
salt and pepper

Wash the chicory, slicing off the bottoms and discarding any wilted outer leaves. Put in a heavy pan with the butter, lemon juice and seasoning. Cover and simmer very slowly for 1 hour.

ENDIVES AU JUS

Ingredients   salt and pepper
8 chicory heads   2 tbsp juices from a roast

Prepare the chicory and boil 10 minutes. Drain and return
to pan with the meat juices and seasoning. Simmer for a
further 5 minutes.

ENDIVES A LA BÉCHAMEL

Ingredients   1 oz flour
8 chicory heads   ½ pint milk
2 oz butter   salt and pepper

Prepare the chicory, and boil 10 minutes. Drain, put in
vegetable dish and cover with a sauce made by melting the
butter, stirring in the flour and seasoning and adding,
gradually, the milk.

ENDIVES AU LARD

(chicory with bacon)

Ingredients   4 shallots
8 chicory heads   8 rashers of streaky bacon
3 oz butter   2 celery stalks

Prepare the chicory, cutting them down the centre
lengthwise. Lightly fry the chopped bacon with the sliced
shallots and celery in 1 oz of the butter. Fill the chicory with
this. Put the remaining 2 oz of butter in an ovenproof dish,
arrange the chicory and bake 45 minutes in a moderate
oven, basting from time to time.

ENDIVES AU GRATIN

(baked chicory)

Ingredients
8 chicory heads   ½ pint milk
2 oz butter   seasoning
1 oz flour   3 oz grated cheese

Prepare and boil the endives. Drain and put in an ovenproof dish. Make a sauce by melting the butter, stirring in the flour and adding, gradually, the milk. Stir until it thickens. Add seasoning and 2 oz of the grated cheese. Pour this sauce over the chicory. Sprinkle with the remaining cheese and bake 10 minutes in a hot oven.

ENDIVES BRAISÉES

Ingredients
8 chicory heads
2 medium-sized carrots
2 onions
2 oz butter
bouquet garni
2 bacon rashers
salt and pepper

Toss the sliced carrots and onions in the butter until soft. Put in the bottom of an ovenproof dish together with the *bouquet garni.* Add the chicory and 2 oz of water and top with the chopped bacon. Cover and bake 45 minutes in a slow oven.

ENDIVES A LA MEUNIÈRE

Ingredients
8 chicory heads
2 oz butter
salt and pepper
flour

Prepare the chicory and boil 10 minutes. Drain well, roll in the seasoned flour and fry on both sides in the butter.

ENDIVES A LA PROVENÇALE

Ingredients
8 chicory heads
4 oz tomato *coulis*
(see page 188)
2 oz Parmesan cheese
2 oz melted butter

Prepare the chicory and boil 10 minutes. Put in an ovenproof dish. Cover with the tomato *coulis* and top with the Parmesan cheese and seasoning. Sprinkle over this the melted butter and bake 5 minutes.

ENDIVES A LA FLAMANDE
(Flemish-style chicory)

Ingredients

8 chicory heads	**juice of a lemon**
4 oz butter	**1 oz flour**
pinch of grated nutmeg	**¼ pint meat stock**
¼ pint water	**¼ pint white wine**

Prepare the chicory and put in pan with 2 oz of the butter, the lemon juice, nutmeg and water. Cook slowly for 30 minutes and drain. Melt the remaining 2 oz of butter, stir in the flour and add the wine and meat stock. Add the chicory and simmer 10 minutes, stirring frequently. Pass through vegetable mill and return to pan with the seasoning to heat through.

LAITUES AU JUS

Ingredients

4 lettuces	**4 onions**
2 oz butter	**2 bacon rashers**
2 tbsp butter	**salt and pepper**
juices from a roast	***croûtons***

In an ovenproof dish put the butter, chopped bacon rashers, sliced onions, salt and pepper. Add the prepared lettuces, cover and bake in a slow oven until tender. Add the meat juices and cook a further 5 minutes. Serve with the *croûtons*.

LAITUES AU BEURRE

Ingredients

4 lettuces, with good-sized hearts	**2 tbsp water**
	bouquet garni
8 small onions	**tsp sugar**
2 oz butter	**salt**

Thoroughly wash the lettuces and put in a pan, squeezing well together, with the butter, water, sugar, salt and *bouquet garni*. Cover and simmer until tender. Remove *bouquet garni* on serving.

LAITUES A LA CRÈME

Ingredients
4 lettuces with good-sized
  hearts
2 oz butter

2 tbsp water
tsp sugar
bouquet garni
2 oz cream

Prepare the lettuces and cook as in above recipe. When tender, remove *bouquet garni* and stir in the cream.

LAITUES FARCIES
(stuffed lettuces)

Ingredients
4 firm lettuces
2 oz butter
salt and pepper

breakfastcup cooked rice
2 tbsp tomato *coulis*
  (see page 188)
2 tbsp juices from a roast

Wash well the lettuces, remove centres, and chop these with the rice, tomato *coulis* and seasoning. In an ovenproof dish put the butter and meat juices and bake 30 minutes in a slow oven.

PISSENLITS AU LARD
(dandelions with bacon)

Ingredients
1 lb tender dandelion
  leaves

4 bacon rashers
2 shallots
salt and pepper

Wash well the dandelion leaves, tearing into small pieces. Put in a pan with the chopped bacon rashers, sliced shallots, seasoning and a cupful of water. Simmer half an hour.

PISSENLITS AU BEURRE

Ingredients
1 lb dandelion leaves
juice of half a lemon

1 cupful white bread-
  crumbs
salt and pepper

Prepare the dandelion leaves and boil in salted water until tender. Drain and return to pan with the butter, breadcrumbs, lemon juice and seasoning. Stir until well blended.

15

TOMATOES

Tomatoes never taste quite so good as when eaten straight off the bush. But since few can enjoy them this way the British cook compromises with salad – an undressed mixture of lettuce, radishes, beetroot and tomatoes. The French cook compromises with a tomato salad accompanied by a French dressing. Sometimes a small tin of tunny fish is added while in southern districts fresh basil often replaces the parsley.

Tomatoes really only began to reach the table during the past century, having for long been considered poisonous, although they had been introduced into Europe two centuries earlier. At first the Italians called them *pomi d'ori*, Latin for 'golden apple' and, technically, they are indeed a fruit. Today the Italian name is still *pomodora*, misinterpreted by our Victorian ancestors as *pomme d'amour*, or love apple, which is probably why it came to be considered an aphrodisiac.

When there is a glut and they are cheap it is wise to bottle them since they are invaluable for soups and sauces, pizzas and cassoulets, pasta and soufflés. Green tomato jam also has its addicts.

A certain variety of yellow tomato occasionally reaches our greengrocers and is delicious as a salad. Its slight acidity dispenses with vinegar in the dressing.

Rich in vitamin C, tomatoes are nevertheless inadvisable for those who suffer from rheumatism.

TOMATES EN HORS D'OEUVRE (1)

Ingredients
4 ripe tomatoes
2 tbsp brown sugar
4 cloves

2 bayleaves
juice of a lemon
2 oz cognac
2 oz cream, seasoning

Plunge the tomatoes into boiling water for a few minutes and skin. In a pan put the pulp, the sugar, cloves, bayleaves, lemon juice, cognac and seasoning. Simmer for 10 minutes. Beat the cream and fold in. Refrigerate and serve in individual glasses topped with a slice each of tomato and lemon.

TOMATES EN HORS D'OEUVRE (2)

Ingredients
4 medium-sized tomatoes
yolk of egg
small tin of tunny fish

1 tsp vinegar seasoning
pinch of mustard powder
lettuce leaves
olive oil as required

Cut tomatoes in halves, scoop out the pulp and mix with the tunny and mayonnaise made as follows: break the egg yolk into a bowl with the mustard powder and beat; add the olive oil, drop by drop, beating all the time; when of a creamy consistency add the vinegar and seasoning. Return the prepared pulp to shells and serve on the lettuce leaves.

TOMATES EN HORS D'OEUVRE (3)

Ingredients
4 medium-sized tomatoes
½ cup chopped mint

1 breakfastcup cooked
  rice
seasoning

Cut tomatoes in halves, scoop out pulp and mix with the rice, mint and seasoning. Return to shells.

SALADE DE TOMATES
(tomato salad)

Ingredients
4 ripe tomatoes
1 tbsp olive oil
1 tsp vinegar

seasoning
1 finely chopped shallot
½ cup chopped parsley

Slice the tomatoes and mix well with the olive oil, vinegar, shallot and seasoning. Garnish with the chopped parsley.

PANIERS DE TOMATES
(tomato baskets)

Ingredients

4 large tomatoes	1 tbsp olive oil
half a cucumber	juice of half a lemon
1 small lettuce	seasoning

Make slits in the tomatoes and into each insert a slice of cucumber. Serve on a bed of lettuce previously dressed with the oil, lemon juice and seasoning.

FLEURS DE TOMATES
(tomato flowers)

Ingredients

4 tomatoes	$\frac{1}{2}$ cup grated celery
2 shallots	$\frac{1}{2}$ cup cooked peas
	$\frac{1}{2}$ cup mayonnaise

Form the tomatoes into flower shapes by slitting downwards from the top so that the skin can be pulled down to form petals. Scoop out the pulp, chop and mix with the celery, peas and well-chopped shallots. Add the mayonnaise (see recipe for tomato hors d'oeuvre (2)). Fill with this mixture.

TOMATES A LA MENTONNAISE

Ingredients

1 small green pepper	1 lb tomatoes
1 celery branch	small tin of anchovy fillets

Remove seeds from pepper, cut up small and boil with the chopped celery for 20 minutes. Allow to cool, season and mix with the sliced tomatoes and anchovy fillets. Refrigerate.

TOMATES AU FROMAGE
(tomatoes with cheese)

Ingredients	1 oz butter
4 medium-sized tomatoes	¼ pint milk
1 egg	salt and pepper
2 oz grated cheese	1 tbsp olive oil

Cut tomatoes in halves, scoop out pulp and mix with scrambled eggs made with the butter, milk and seasoning. Top each with the grated cheese. Cover the bottom of an ovenproof dish with the oil. Arrange the tomatoes and bake about 20 minutes in a moderate oven, until cheese is golden.

TOMATES FARCIES AU RIZ
(rice-stuffed tomatoes)

Ingredients	
4 medium-sized tomatoes	½ pint meat stock
2 oz margarine	¼ lb mushrooms
breakfastcup rice	seasoning

Slice tops off the tomatoes, remove and discard pulp and bake 10 minutes. Melt the margarine, add the rice and sliced mushrooms and stir until rice is golden. Add the stock, a little at a time, and continue cooking until the rice has absorbed all the liquid. Season and stuff the tomatoes with this mixture. Put in a well-greased ovenproof dish and bake 10 minutes.

TOMATES MONAGASQUES

Ingredients	2 garlic cloves
1 breakfastcup white	herbs as available
breadcrumbs	1 oz olive oil
4 large tomatoes	pepper
cupful milk	2 oz grated Parmesan
2 anchovy fillets	cheese

Slice off tops from the tomatoes and remove, carefully, the pulp. Put tomato shells on a plate in a moderate oven for 5 minutes. Drain. Make a stuffing of the breadcrumbs previously soaked in the milk and squeezed out, and the well-chopped garlic and anchovy fillets. Stuff the tomatoes with this mixture. Cover the bottom of an ovenproof dish with the olive oil. Put in the tomatoes, sprinkle with the Parmesan cheese and bake 20 minutes in a moderate oven.

PAIN DE TOMATES
(tomato loaf)

Ingredients

½ lb ripe tomatoes	2 oz grated cheese
2 eggs	mustard powder
2 cups breadcrumbs	salt
½ pint milk	tsp paprika

Plunge the tomatoes into boiling water, drain and remove skins. Mash the pulp. Warm the milk and beat in the eggs. Add the breadcrumbs, the grated cheese, pinch of mustard powder, salt and paprika to the pulp. Put this mixture into a well-greased ovenproof dish and bake in a moderate oven until set.

TOMATES AU GRATIN
(baked tomatoes)

Ingredients

4 large tomatoes	garlic salt
1 cup chopped parsley	pepper
2 shallots	browned breadcrumbs

Slice the tops off the tomatoes, scoop out the pulp and mix with the parsley, finely chopped shallots, garlic salt and pepper. Return to shells and top with the breadcrumbs. Cover the bottom of an ovenproof dish with the oil. Arrange the tomatoes and bake 15 minutes in a moderate oven.

MOUSSE DE TOMATES

Ingredients

1 lb tomatoes	salt and pepper
2 oz powdered gelatine	2 tbsp white wine
	2 oz cream

Skin the tomatoes and sieve. Dissolve the gelatine in the wine and add, together with the seasoning. Stir in the cream. Put in a mould, previously rinsed out with cold water, and turn out when set.

SOUFFLÉ DE TOMATES

Ingredients	¼ pint milk
1 lb ripe tomatoes	4 eggs
1 oz olive oil	seasoning
1 oz butter	2 oz grated Parmesan
½ oz flour	cheese

Scoop out the pulp of the tomatoes and fry gently in the olive oil until reduced to a purée. Meanwhile heat the butter, add the flour and, gradually, the milk. Stir till it thickens. Remove from heat and beat in the egg yolks, Parmesan, seasoning and tomato pulp. Whisk egg whites until stiff and fold in. Pour into a buttered soufflé dish and bake 20 minutes in a hot oven.

TOMATES RISSOLÉES
(tomato rissoles)

Ingredients	1 egg
1 lb tomatoes	seasoning
1 oz olive oil	4 oz Quaker Oats
1 tsp mixed herbs	flour
2 shallots	2 oz margarine

Put the tomatoes in boiling water for a few seconds. Drain and remove skins. Put in a pan with the olive oil together with the herbs and sliced shallots and simmer gently until reduced to a purée. Remove from heat and stir in the well-beaten egg, seasoning and Quaker Oats. Leave for an hour. Then shape into rissoles, roll in the flour and fry. Serve with a green salad.

TOMATES A LA CRÈME

Ingredients	thyme
4 ripe tomatoes	basil
1 oz olive oil	parsley
1 large onion	2 oz cream

Cut the tomatoes into halves. Heat the olive oil and fry the sliced onion until soft and yellow. Add the tomatoes, cut sides uppermost, and sprinkle with the herbs. Continue cooking gently, stir in the cream and serve immediately.

TOMATES FERMIER
(farmhouse-style tomatoes)

Ingredients	2 slices chopped ham
4 tomatoes	seasoning
2 oz butter	3 eggs

Slice the tomatoes and put in pan with the butter, ham and seasoning. Simmer for 5 minutes. Beat well the eggs and add, stirring until it begins to set. Serve on toast.

OMELETTES DE TOMATES

Ingredients	4 ripe tomatoes
1 oz olive oil	seasoning
4 oz mushrooms	4 eggs
2 cloves garlic	2 oz butter

Heat the olive oil and fry, gently, the sliced mushrooms and garlic until soft. Scoop out the pulp from the tomatoes and add, together with the seasoning. Continue to let this simmer while making the omelettes with the butter and eggs. Fill each omelette with the tomato mixture and fold over.

TOMATES AUX CHAMPIGNONS
(tomatoes with mushrooms)

Ingredients	2 shallots
4 large tomatoes	1 cup breadcrumbs
1 oz butter	salt and pepper
¼ lb mushrooms	2 oz sour cream

Cut off the tops from the tomatoes and scoop out the pulp. In the butter gently fry the sliced mushrooms and shallots until transparent. Add breadcrumbs, seasoning and cream and fill the tomatoes with this mixture. Cover with the tops, put in an ovenproof dish, having covered the bottom with a little olive oil, and bake 20 minutes in a slow oven.

BEIGNETS DE TOMATES
(tomato fritters)

Ingredients

2 oz flour	salt and pepper
1 egg	4 firm tomatoes
½ pint milk	3 oz olive oil

Make a batter mixture by putting the flour in a bowl, breaking in the egg and adding, gradually, the milk. Season. Slice the tomatoes, dip in the batter mixture and fry in the sizzling hot oil.

RAGOÛT DE TOMATES
(stewed tomatoes)

Ingredients

2 oz butter	seasoning
4 shallots	1 oz flour
2 rashers of streaky bacon	12 de-stoned black olives
8 small tomatoes	2 oz white wine

Heat the butter and gently fry the chopped shallots and bacon rashers. Cut the tomatoes in quarters and add, together with the seasoning, flour, olives and wine. Simmer gently for a further 10 minutes.

TOMATES A LA PROVENÇALE
(Provençal-style tomatoes)

Ingredients

4 good-sized tomatoes	flesh of 1 eggplant
4 oz rice	2 garlic cloves
2 tbsp olive oil	salt and pepper
	½ pint water

Halve the tomatoes and remove the pulp. Heat the olive oil, add the rice and cook until it turns yellow but not brown. Add the flesh of the eggplant, the chopped garlic and the tomato pulp. Add seasoning and the water and simmer until all the water is absorbed. Fill the tomatoes with this mixture, put into an oiled ovenproof dish and cook in a moderate oven.

CONFITURE DE TOMATES
(green tomato jam)

Ingredients
4lb green tomatoes juice of 2 lemons
2 oz ginger 5 lb sugar

Dice the tomatoes and put in pan together with the ginger and lemon juice. Bring very slowly to the boil. Add the sugar and boil fast for 20 minutes or until set. Pour into previously prepared jars and seal.

16

SALADS

As I explained in the Introduction, in France a number of vegetables are served on their own in the form of salads. Hence the recipes for these have already been given; whereas they take the form of an hors d'oeuvre, the green salads given here are occasionally served with the main course but most usually after it.

There are, of course, mixed salads always served as an hors d'oeuvre, such as *salade niçoise* and *crudités*, the latter often to be seen on restaurant menus: it simply means a number of raw vegetables, each in its own separate dish and with its own dressing, such as grated carrot, mushrooms, cucumber and tomato. But never that mixture of lettuce, tomato, cucumber and radishes that in Britain is so often produced if one asks for a salad. Radishes, in fact, should always be served on their own since their strong flavour kills that of other vegetables.

Salad combinations are numerous, and remember when composing one that rice is an excellent ingredient.

Lettuce, of which there are some fifty species, is to be found throughout the temperate regions of the northern hemisphere. Best known is garden lettuce, which was known to the ancient Greeks and Romans and which has been grown in Britain at least since Elizabethan times.

The leaves should be left whole or torn, but never cut (except in the case of chicory) since this bruises them. They should be washed quickly and drained in a salad basket or cloth before dressing.

The base of this dressing is a fatty substance and an acid. The former can be olive or other oil or cream, the acid either wine vinegar or lemon juice. Malt vinegar is worse than useless. Grapefruit juice can also be used. The proportions are one part acid to three or four of oil or cream.

The salt and pepper should be diluted with the vinegar in the salad bowl before adding the oil as they dissolve in vinegar but not in oil.

Vegetable salads and the tougher ones such as chicory and dandelion should be tossed with the dressing half an hour before serving in order that the dressing has the time to penetrate. Delicate green salads such as lettuce, watercress and lambs' lettuce, should be dressed at the last minute and the quantity of vinegar reduced. For those who like a hint of garlic, the bowl should be rubbed round with a cut clove.

An alternative to French dressing is an egg yolk beaten with olive oil, as for mayonnaise, and the addition of mustard powder, herbs, salt and pepper diluted with a teaspoon of hot water. Another alternative is sour cream or yoghourt combined with lemon juice, mustard powder, a pinch of sugar, salt and pepper.

For variety, chopped walnuts, chopped celery, slivers of red pepper and fennel, chives, chopped onion or shallots all go well with green salads. So, too, do cubes of Gruyère cheese.

One of the most delicious of winter salads, and often neglected in British gardens, is the little lambs' lettuce, sometimes known as corn or winter salad.

Ignored, too, although very popular in France, are young dandelion leaves, so easily available in the spring particularly in the country where people go out to pick the youngest plants which are the most tender. Only the white leaves should be used and for those who find the flavour slightly too bitter they can be mixed with other salads.

Watercress, too, is seldom used except as a garnish, yet is of considerable medical value as well as making an excellent salad.

Wine should never be drunk with salad on account of the vinegar usually contained in the dressing and also because of the very nature of a green salad. But as in France it is served between the meat and cheese courses this causes no undue inconvenience.

LAITUE EN SALADE
(lettuce salad)

Ingredients	3 tbsp olive oil
1 good-sized lettuce	1 dsp wine vinegar
1 shallot	salt and pepper

Wash the lettuce in several lots of water, discarding any wilted outer leaves; divide into bite-sized pieces and drain. In salad bowl mix the seasoning with the vinegar and stir in the olive oil. Add the finely chopped shallot and the lettuce and toss well. Serve immediately.

SALADE DE SCAROLE
(salad of curly endive)

Ingredients	2 eggs
2 curly endives	pinch of mustard powder
3 tbsp olive oil ·	¼ cup chopped tarragon
1 dsp wine vinegar	and chervil
1 shallot	salt and pepper

Hard boil the eggs and remove shells. Prepare the endive, drain and toss in a dressing made with the oil, vinegar, mustard and seasoning. Add the herbs and chopped shallot and decorate with the sliced hardboiled eggs.

LAITUE A LA CRÈME

Ingredients	2 oz cream
1 large lettuce	juice of half a lemon
2 egg yolks	salt

Prepare the lettuce and drain. Put the cream and egg yolks in a pan on very low heat, whipping with a fork until well blended. Add salt. Leave to cool and add the lemon juice. Toss lettuce in this dressing.

SALADE ROMAINE
(cos lettuce salad)

Ingredients	2 fennel stalks
1 good-sized cos lettuce	3 tbsp olive oil
4 anchovy fillets	1 tbsp vinegar

Wash the lettuce in several lots of water and drain. In salad bowl mix the vinegar, and chopped anchovy fillets. Blend in the oil and add the chopped fennel and lettuce. Toss well half an hour before serving.

ROMAINE AUX AMANDES
(cos lettuce with almonds)

Ingredients

1 good-sized cos lettuce	pinch of mustard powder
3 tbsp olive oil	cupful salted almonds
juice of half a lemon	pepper

Prepare the lettuce and drain. Half an hour before serving mix in salad bowl the lemon juice, pepper and mustard powder. Blend in the oil. Add the lettuce and almonds and toss well.

LAITUE AUX POIVRONS
(lettuce with peppers)

Ingredients

1 good-sized lettuce	2 tbsp olive oil
1 small red pepper	1 tsp wine vinegar
yolk of an egg	salt and pepper

Prepare the lettuce and drain. Wash the pepper, removing all seeds, and chop small. In salad bowl mix the vinegar and seasoning. Blend in the oil and add the pepper and lettuce. Toss well. Mince the egg yolk and sprinkle over the lettuce. Serve immediately.

SCAROLE AU ROQUEFORT
(curly endive with blue cheese)

Ingredients

2 curly-leaved endives	½ cup chopped walnuts
1 tbsp wine vinegar	3 tbsp olive oil
pinch of Cayenne pepper	1 oz Roquefort or other
	blue cheese

Prepare the endives and leave to drain. Half an hour before serving put the cheese into salad bowl and blend well

with the vinegar and pepper. Blend in the oil. Add the
endives and walnuts and toss well.

SALADE DE MÂCHE
(lambs' lettuce salad)

Ingredients	tarragon and chives,
¼ lb lambs' lettuce	chopped small
1 medium-sized cooked	3 tbsp olive oil
beetroot	1 dsp vinegar
¼ cup chervil	salt and pepper

Wash the lettuce in several lots of water, removing the
bottom of each tuft and any yellow leaves. Drain. In salad
bowl mix the vinegar, herbs and seasoning. Blend in the oil
and, just before serving, the cubed beetroot and lettuce.
Toss well.

SALADE DE CRESSON
(watercress salad)

Ingredients	
bunch of watercress	1 tbsp wine vinegar
3 tbsp olive oil	salt and pepper

Wash the watercress, removing the hard stalks. Drain.
Half an hour before serving mix the vinegar and seasoning
in salad bowl. Blend in the oil. Add the watercress and toss
well.

CRESSON AU PAMPLEMOUSSE
(watercress with grapefruit)

Ingredients	
1 bunch of watercress	3 tbsp olive oil
half a grapefruit	salt and pepper

Prepare the watercress and drain. Remove pith and pips
from the grapefruit and chop the segments. In salad bowl
mix these with the seasoning. Blend in the olive oil. Add the
watercress and toss well.

PISSENLITS AUX LARDONS
(dandelion salad)

Ingredients

¼ lb dandelion leaves
4 rashers streaky bacon

3 tbsp olive oil
1 tbsp wine vinegar
salt and pepper

Wash well the dandelion leaves and drain. Fry the bacon rashers lightly and chop small. When cold, mix in salad bowl, the vinegar and seasoning. Blend in the oil. Add the dandelion leaves and bacon half an hour before serving, tossing well.

ENDIVES EN SALADE
(chicory salad)

Ingredients

2 heads chicory
2 oz Gruyère or other
   hard cheese

3 tbsp olive oil
1 tbsp wine vinegar
tbsp chopped chives
salt and pepper

Cut the cheese into small cubes. Wash the chicory, removing the hard centres. Half an hour before serving mix, in salad bowl, the seasoning and vinegar. Blend in the olive oil. Add the chopped chicory, chives and cheese. Toss well.

ENDIVES A L'AIL
(chicory with garlic)

Ingredients

2 heads chicory
3 garlic cloves
3 tbsp olive oil
1 tbsp vinegar

breakfastcupful of crusts
   from a loaf of French
   bread
salt and pepper

Prepare the chicory and drain. Cut the bread crust into cubes and rub these with a cut garlic clove. Also rub round the salad bowl. Mince the garlic. In salad bowl mix the vinegar and seasoning. Blend in the oil. An hour before serving add the chopped chicory, bread cubes and garlic, turning at intervals so that the garlic flavour is thoroughly integrated.

ENDIVES A LA MAYONNAISE

Ingredients

2 heads chicory	tsp of vinegar
pinch of mustard powder	olive oil
salt and pepper	1 egg yolk

Prepare the chicory and drain. Make a mayonnaise by putting the egg yolk into a basin with the mustard powder and beat. Add the oil, drop by drop, beating all the time until a creamy consistency is obtained. Add the vinegar and seasoning. Mix in the salad bowl with the chopped chicory.

CRUDITÉS A LA PROVENÇALE
(uncooked vegetable salad)

Ingredients

3 medium-sized young carrots	2 sticks celery
¼ lb mushrooms	half a red pepper
breakfastcupful peeled and sliced cucumber	1 tbsp chopped basil
	tsp capers
2 anchovy fillets	12 de-stoned black olives
heart of a fennel	½ pint tomato *coulis* (see page 188)

Prepare the vegetables, first washing, then grating the raw carrots, slicing the mushrooms and chopping small the celery, fennel and pepper, having removed seeds from the latter. Mix with the capers, basil, chopped anchovy fillets and olives and blend all together with the tomato *coulis*.

SALADE D'HIVER
(mixed winter salad)

Ingredients

1 medium-sized cooked beetroot	tsp vinegar
3 Cox's orange pippins	pinch of mustard powder
half a small celeriac	1 egg yolk
1 head chicory	olive oil
	salt and pepper

Prepare the chicory and drain. Dice the beetroot and put to soak in vinegar for 2 hours. Peel and core the apples and cut into cubes. Peel the celeriac and slice. Drain the beetroot and put into salad bowl with the chopped chicory, celeriac and apples. Make a mayonnaise as in recipe for chicory and mix this well with the vegetables.

VERDURETTE
(mixed green salad)

Ingredients

cupful young spinach leaves	1 tbsp each chopped parsley, tarragon and chervil
heart of a white cabbage	1 cup peeled and sliced cucumber
½ cup radish leaves	
1 small curly endive	1 tbsp vinegar
3 tbsp olive oil	salt and pepper

Wash well the spinach, cabbage, endive and radish leaves. Drain and chop. In salad bowl mix the seasoning with the vinegar. Blend in the oil. Add the prepared salad and herbs and toss well. Leave for half an hour before serving.

BASÇONNAISE
(raw vegetable salad from the Basque country)

Ingredients

4 carrots	3 tomatoes
1 small parsnip	1 small red cabbage
1 medium-sized beetroot	½ cup mixed herbs
¼ lb mushrooms	3 tbsp olive oil
2 shallots	1 tbsp vinegar
2 celery stalks	salt and pepper

Scrub, peel and grate the carrots, beetroot, parsnip and mushrooms. Chop small the shallots and celery. Shred the cabbage and slice the tomatoes. Put the vinegar and seasoning in salad bowl and blend in the oil. Half an hour before serving add the vegetables and the herbs and mix well.

SALADE BEAUCAIRE

Ingredients

2 stalks celery	tsp mustard powder
1 small celeriac	1 egg yolk
2 chicory heads	½ teaspoon Cayenne
2 small beetroot	pepper
12 de-stoned green olives	olive oil
juice of a lemon	salt

Chop small the celery stalks, dice the beetroot, grate the celeriac and chop the prepared chicory. Make a dressing with 2 tablespoons olive oil, the lemon juice, salt and Cayenne. Soak the vegetables in this dressing for 2 hours, turning occasionally. Make a mayonnaise as in recipe for chicory, omitting the vinegar and noting the larger quantity of mustard powder.

SALADE DES GOBELINS

Ingredients	salt
1 lb potatoes	pinch of Cayenne pepper
2 celery stalks	1 dsp wine vinegar
hearts of 2 artichokes	4 oz cream
1 oz finely sliced truffles	1 dsp chopped chives

Boil the potatoes in their skins and peel. Wash and chop the celery. While the potatoes are still warm mix them with the celery, artichoke slices, salt, Cayenne and vinegar. When cold blend in the cream and sprinkle with the chives and truffles.

SALADE NIÇOISE

Ingredients	hearts of 2 lettuces
2 eggs	small tin of tunny fish
4 tomatoes	3 tbsp olive oil
1 cup black olives	1 tbsp wine vinegar
4 anchovy fillets	salt and pepper

Hard boil the eggs, shell and slice. Mix together the seasoning and vinegar in salad bowl and blend in the oil.

Half an hour before serving mix in the sliced eggs and tomatoes, the shredded lettuces, chopped anchovy fillets, olives and tunny fish.

SALADE JURASSIENNE

(salad of cauliflower and haricot beans)

Ingredients	2 oz Gruyère cheese
1 small cauliflower	4 tbsp olive oil
1 lb green haricot beans	2 tsp vinegar
1 egg	salt and pepper

Divide the cauliflower into florets and boil 10 minutes in salted water. Drain. Prepare the beans and boil 20 minutes with a pinch of bicarbonate of soda. Drain. Hard boil the eggs. An hour before serving mix 2 tbsp of the olive oil with 1 tsp of vinegar and seasoning. Mix in the beans. Put the cauliflower florets in the centre of a dish. Make a dressing with the remaining 2 tbsp of olive oil and remaining tea-spoon of vinegar, the minced egg and seasoning. Pour this over the cauliflower. Add the diced cheese to the beans and arrange then around the cauliflower.

SALADE TALLEYRAND

Ingredients	2 carrots
1 breakfastcup rice	salt and pepper
2 breakfastcups shelled	3 tbsp olive oil
peas	1 tbsp vinegar

Cook the rice by boiling fast for 8 minutes. Drain. Wash and peel the carrots. Boil and pass through vegetable mill. Half an hour before serving mix, in the salad bowl, the vinegar and seasoning. Blend in the oil and add the rice, peas and carrots.

SALADE CATALANE

Ingredients	2 anchovy fillets
3 large onions	3 tbsp olive oil
1 small red pepper	1 tbsp wine vinegar

Cook the prepared onions in the oven in a minimum of water. Drain and dice. Cut the pepper in halves, removing seeds, and grill on both sides. Dice. Chop the anchovy fillets. Half an hour before serving put the anchovy fillets and pepper in salad bowl with the oil. Blend well and add the onions and pepper.

SALADE PAYSANNE

Ingredients
¼ lb dandelion leaves
½ lb tomatoes
2 shallots
cupful chopped walnuts
cupful peeled and sliced
   cucumber
3 tbsp olive oil
1 tbsp wine vinegar
salt and pepper

Wash well the dandelion leaves and drain. Slice the tomatoes and chop the shallots. In salad bowl mix the salt and pepper with the vinegar. Blend in the oil and add the dandelion leaves, shallots, cucumber, tomatoes and walnuts. Toss well.

SALADE DE BETTERAVES ET CHAMPIGNONS
(beetroot and mushroom salad)

Ingredients
2 medium-sized beetroot
½ lb mushrooms
1 egg yolk
1 tsp vinegar
pinch of mustard powder
olive oil
salt and pepper

Prepare and boil the beetroot. Drain and dice. Scrub the mushrooms, boil 10 minutes and slice. Make a mayonnaise as in *endives à la mayonnaise* (see page 165) and mix well with the beetroot and mushrooms.

SALADE DE TOMATES ET AVOCAT
(tomato and avocado salad)

Ingredients
1 ripe avocado pear
3 medium-sized tomatoes
2 onions
tsp each of paprika,
   salt and lemon juice
1 tsp vinegar

Slice the tomatoes and marinate in the oil and vinegar for half an hour. Slice the onions into rings. Peel and dice the avocado pear and put in a bowl with the salt. paprika and lemon juice. Arrange the tomato slices round the outside of serving dish, overlap with the onion rings and in the centre put the prepared avocado pear.

SALADE PANACHÉE
(mixed salad)

Ingredients

2 small beetroot	1 tbsp chopped tarragon
1 small celeriac	4 medium-sized potatoes
3 Cox's orange pippins	yolk of an egg
1 tbsp chopped chervil	1 tsp vinegar
	olive oil

Boil and peel the beetroot. Drain and dice. Boil the potatoes until cooked but still firm. Peel. core and dice the apples. Peel and grate the celeriac. Make a mayonnaise as in *endives à la mayonnaise* and mix well with the prepared vegetables, chervil and tarragon. Leave half an hour before serving.

SALADE BAGUARETTE

Ingredients

2 cups broccoli florets	salt and pepper
1 small white cabbage	pinch of mustard powder
2 celery stalks	2 dsp tomato ketchup
half a small red pepper	1 tsp cream
yolk of an egg	1 tsp Worcester Sauce
olive oil	salt and pepper

Boil the broccoli in salted water for 5 minutes and drain. Chop the celery stalks and the pepper. Shred the cabbage. Make a mayonnaise as *endives à la mayonnaise,* replacing the vinegar by the Worcester Sauce. Blend in the cream and ketchup and mix well with the prepared vegetables.

SALADE EN GELÉE

(salad in aspic)

Ingredients
half a green pepper
1 finely chopped shallot
3 medium-sized tomatoes
½ pint meat stock
1 oz powdered gelatine
salt and pepper
1 tsp chopped basil
1 head of chicory
salt and pepper
2 tbsp olive oil
1 tsp vinegar

Boil the pepper for 5 minutes, drain and chop. Plunge the tomatoes into boiling water, remove skins and mash. Heat the meat stock and in it dissolve the gelatine. When on the point of setting add to the tomatoes, pepper, shallot, basil and seasoning. Put into a ring, previously rinsed out in cold water. Unmould when set and in centre arrange the chopped chicory, previously tossed in the oil, vinegar and seasoning.

17

SAUCES

The great statesman Talleyrand once said that England had three sauces and three hundred and sixty religions whereas France had three religions and three hundred and sixty sauces.

There are many other adages about sauces, such as *'A bonne viande – courte sauce'* meaning that good quality meat needs only a minimum of sauce; *'la sauce fait passer le poisson'*, that it is the sauce which facilitates the consumption of fish, and *'une sauce doit prolonger le goût d'un plat mais jamais le masquer'*, that a sauce should bring out the flavour of a dish but never mask it.

Here, however, we are concerned only with those sauces in which herbs and vegetables are part of the ingredients, and there are an appreciable number, many of them making an excellent accompaniment to meat and fish.

Without knowing which three sauces Talleyrand was referring to, one can nevertheless make a good guess since the British housewife still seems to rely on gravy to accompany meat, a white sauce for fish and bottled mayonnaise for cold dishes.

Yet although it is certainly true that the sauce should never mask the flavour of a dish, there is no doubt that a good sauce works wonders for poor quality meat or insipid fish.

So much has been written about the magic of sauces that the impression is often given that they belong to the realm of *haute cuisine* and are therefore too complicated for the home cook to master; an impression enforced by yet another adage, that *'la cuisine avec des sauces devient de la gastronomie',* that sauces turn cooking into gastronomy. But in fact sauces are really indispensable to good cooking and are often part of the dishes themselves. So that the more one knows about their preparation, the greater the variety of one's cooking.

The blending of a sauce is particularly important. An egg yolk is often used to thicken, giving a better texture and with less chance of becoming lumpy. When this is used the sauce should never be allowed to boil.

The tasting of the sauce is also important, particularly to test whether the seasoning is correct.

When boiling vegetables the cooking water should always be preserved for stock, providing a useful base for a number of sauces.

Mirepoix and tomato *coulis* are also a basis for other sauces, both of which can be stored. While for cold dishes there are several variations of mayonnaise.

Mayonnaise, incidentally, is a deformed form of its original name of *mahonnaise,* created in honour of the victory of Maréchal de Richelieu at Port-Mahon, while *sauce béarnaise* was invented in 1860 by a Béarnais chef of the celebrated Pavillon Henri IV at St. Germain-en-Laye.

Since it is helpful to have an idea of the uses of the most important of these sauces, it should be remembered that *sauce maître d'hôtel* goes well with fish, meat, liver and vegetables; Madeira sauce with kidneys, roast beef, braised chicory and mushrooms; *sauce gribiche* with green salads, cold fish and seafood; *sauce tartare* also goes well with cold fish and seafood while *sauce Bretonne* is preferable for hot fish. *Sauce bordelaise* accompanies beef; *sauce chasseur* rabbit and veal. Veal is also good with tomato sauce which also accompanies pasta and eggs. *Sauce lyonnaise* is served with all meat dishes, particularly tripe, and with vegetables. Barbecue sauce goes well with grills as well as with a *fondue bourguignonne.* Also good with grills are *sauce béarnaise, sauce provençale* and *herb sauce,* the latter also good for omelettes, pasta and rice. *Sauce piquante* is served with tongue and calves' heads; olive sauce with duck, veal and game; truffle sauce with game and roasts. *Sauce duxelle* goes well with white meat and baked dishes, tarragon sauce with cold meat and fish while *mayonnaise verte* is served with cold veal, fish and asparagus. Parsley butter accompanies grills and fish; basil butter grills, pasta and rice; *beurre ravigote* grilled fish and meat, and *beurre de poivron* is used for canapés. Also served on canapés is *ouillade,* a walnut spread, and *tapenade,* a spread of black olives and capers, the name being derived from the Provençal *tapeno,* meaning capers. Onion sauce is popular in France as well as in Britain with mutton, but it is also served with chicken and eggs. Sage sauce makes a change from sage and onion stuffing with pork and also with rabbit. Good, too, with pork is *sauce charcutiere* (or *Robert)* as well as with poultry, especially pigeons. It is also used to heat up left-over meat with the addition of chopped gherkins. Probably the best known of all regional sauces is *aioli,* or garlic mayonnaise, so evocative of Provençal gastronomy. It is most often encountered with fish, but can also accompany cold meat, vegetables, both cooked and raw, hardboiled eggs and a leg of lamb.

AIOLI

(garlic mayonnaise)

Ingredients
5 garlic cloves
yolks of 2 eggs
juice of half a lemon
salt and pepper
olive oil

Pound the garlic in a mortar and put into a bowl. Add the egg yolks, beating well, and then the olive oil, drop by drop, until a creamy consistency is obtained. Add the lemon juice and seasoning.

BARBECUE SAUCE

Ingredients
¼ lb mushrooms
2 garlic cloves
2 large ripe tomatoes
3 onions
1 tbsp olive oil
¼ pint white wine
1 tsp cornflour
2 tbsp cranberry sauce
1 dsp honey
2 tbsp wine vinegar
1 tsp mustard powder
sprigs of thyme
a bay leaf
few drops tabasco
seasoning

First make a tomato sauce by lightly frying the sliced mushrooms, onions and garlic in the oil. Add the crushed tomatoes and simmer a further two minutes. Stir in the cornflour and honey and add the vinegar, wine, mustard, herbs, seasoning and cranberry sauce. Simmer a further ten minutes and add the tabasco.

SAUCE AURORE

Ingredients
2 oz butter
1 oz flour

¼ pint white wine
2 tbsp tomato purée
seasoning

Melt the butter, stir in the flour and add, gradually, the white wine. Stir until it thickens. Add the seasoning and tomato purée and blend well.

SAUCE BÉARNAISE

Ingredients
¼ pint white wine
2 shallots
yolks of 4 eggs
1 oz butter

1 tsp lemon juice
salt and pepper
1 tbsp chopped parsley
1 tbsp chopped tarragon

Put the chopped shallots into a pan with the wine and boil fast until reduced to two-thirds. Strain. Have ready in a bowl the egg yolks and butter. Pour the sauce over this, return to pan and cook gently, stirring all the time, until it thickens, but never allowing to boil. Add the tarragon, parsley and lemon juice and blend well.

SAUCE BERCY

Ingredients
3 shallots
2 oz butter
juice of half a lemon

salt and pepper
¼ pint white wine
1 tbsp finely chopped parsley

Put all the ingredients into a pan, bring to the boil and simmer 10 minutes.

BEURRE DE BASILIC
(basil butter)

Ingredients

1 cup finely chopped basil leaves

4 oz butter

salt and pepper

Pound together the butter, basil, salt and pepper and stand for 2 hours before serving.

BEURRE DE PERSIL
(parsley butter)

Ingredients

¼ cup finely chopped parsley

4 oz butter

few drops of lemon juice

salt and pepper

Pound together the parsley, butter, seasoning and lemon juice. Stand for 2 hours before serving.

BEURRE DE POIVRON
(sweet pepper butter)

Ingredients

1 small red pepper

4 oz butter

salt

Peel the pepper, removing seeds, and boil 5 minutes. Pass through vegetable mill and pound with the butter and seasoning. Refrigerate.

BEURRE RAVIGOTE

Ingredients

4 oz butter

1 tsp chopped chervil

1 tsp chopped tarragon

1 tbsp chopped watercress

1 tsp chopped chives

salt and pepper

Pound together the butter, herbs and seasoning and stand for 2 hours before serving.

SAUCE BORDELAISE

Ingredients

¼ pint red wine
¼ pint meat stock
1 tbsp olive oil
2 large mushrooms

3 shallots
1 oz tomato purée
1 tsp flour
salt and pepper

Chop finely the mushrooms and shallots and fry lightly in the oil. Stir in the flour and add the wine and stock. Boil until reduced by a third. Blend in the tomato purée and seasoning.

SAUCE BRETONNE

Ingredients

yolks of 2 eggs
juice of half a lemon
olive oil
1 tbsp chopped chives

1 tbsp mixed herbs as
    available
1 tsp mustard powder
salt and pepper

Make a mayonnaise by putting the egg yolks in a bowl with the mustard powder and beating. Add the oil, drop by drop, beating all the time until a creamy consistency is obtained. Add the lemon juice, seasoning and herbs. Blend well.

SAUCE AU CÉLERI

(celery sauce)

Ingredients

the best part of one head
    of celery
2 oz butter

1 oz flour
salt and pepper
1 shallot

Wash and chop the celery and put in a pan with the chopped shallot and half a pint of water. Simmer until tender. Sieve, saving the liquid. Melt the butter, stir in the flour and add, gradually, the cooking water. Stir until it thickens and blend in the sieved celery and seasoning.

SAUCE CHARCUTIÈRE
(also called Sauce Robert)

Ingredients

4 shallots
1 oz butter
1 dsp flour
¼ pint white wine
1 soupspoon wine vinegar

1 tsp mustard powder
1 tbsp chopped gherkins
1 tbsp tomato *coulis* (see
    page 188)
salt and pepper

Slice the shallots and fry lightly in the butter until yellow. Stir in the flour and add the wine, vinegar and seasoning. Simmer 10 minutes. Blend in the mustard and gherkins.

SAUCE CHASSEUR

Ingredients

2 shallots
2 large mushrooms
1 large carrot
¼ pint meat stock
1 tbsp vinegar

2 garlic cloves
1 tbsp juices from a roast
1 oz butter
yolk of an egg
salt and pepper

Scrub and slice the shallots and mushrooms, dice the carrots and garlic and put the vegetables in a pan with the meat stock and vinegar. Simmer until tender and sieve. Return to pan with the butter, seasoning and meat juices. Heat through and, off the heat, blend in the egg yolk.

SAUCE AU CONCOMBRE
(cucumber sauce)

Ingredients

1 small cucumber
meat stock
1 onion
¼ pint milk
2 oz butter

1 oz flour
1 oz cream
salt
pinch of Cayenne pepper
pinch of nutmeg

Peel and slice the cucumber and put in a pan with sufficient meat stock to cover. Bring to the boil, simmer 10 minutes and sieve. Melt the butter, stir in the flour and add, gradually, the milk and cucumber together with the liquid in which it was cooked. Add seasoning and nutmeg and blend in the cream.

SAUCE DIABLE

Ingredients
¼ pint white wine
2 shallots

2 tbsp juices from a roast
pinch of Cayenne pepper
1 tsp mustard powder

Slice the shallots and boil in the wine until the latter is reduced by two thirds. Add the meat juices, pepper and mustard powder and simmer a further 2 minutes.

SAUCE DUXELLE

Ingredients
2 oz butter
1 oz flour
¼ pint white wine

¼ lb mushrooms
2 shallots
1 dsp tomato purée

Boil the sliced mushrooms and shallots in the wine until reduced by two thirds. In a separate pan melt the butter, stir in the flour and add the wine, mushrooms and shallots. Simmer a further 2 minutes.

SAUCE AU FENOUIL
(fennel sauce)

Ingredients
1 dsp chopped fennel
2 oz butter

1 oz flour
¼ pint milk
salt and pepper

Melt the butter, stir in the flour and add, gradually, the milk. Stir until it thickens and add the fennel and seasoning.

SAUCE GRIBICHE

Ingredients
3 eggs
1 tsp mustard powder

olive oil
salt and pepper
1 tbsp mixed herbs

Hard boil two of the eggs, remove the yolks and pound these in a bowl with the yolk of the remaining egg. Add the oil, drop by drop, as for a mayonnaise. Lastly add the vinegar, herbs and seasoning.

SAUCE AUX HERBES
(herb sauce)

Ingredients

2 garlic cloves
2 onions
2 tomatoes
3 tbsp olive oil

1 tbsp each chopped
  tarragon, chervil,
  parsley and chives
salt and pepper

Chop finely the onions, tomatoes and garlic and put them into a pan with the herbs, oil and seasoning. Simmer 10 minutes and refrigerate until ready for use.

SAUCE LYONNAISE

Ingredients

2 onions
1 oz butter
1 tsp vinegar

¼ pint white wine
2 tbsp juices from a roast
salt and pepper

Slice the onions and simmer in the wine and vinegar until reduced by half. Add the meat juices, seasoning and butter, and simmer a further 2 minutes.

SAUCE MADÈRE
(Madeira sauce)

Ingredients

¼ lb mushrooms
¼ pint white wine
2 oz butter

1 oz flour
2 tbsp Madeira wine
salt and pepper

Scrub and slice the mushrooms and boil in just sufficient water to cover for 5 minutes. In a separate pan melt the butter, stir in the flour and add, gradually, the wine, mushrooms with their cooking water and seasoning. Simmer a further 2 minutes and add the Madeira, blending well.

MAYONNAISE DE BETTERAVE
(beetroot mayonnaise)

Ingredients

yolks of 2 eggs
juice of half a lemon

1 small beetroot
pinch of mustard powder
salt and pepper

Scrub the beetroot, peel and shred. Make a mayonnaise by putting the egg yolks in a bowl with the mustard powder and beating. Add the oil, drop by drop, until a creamy consistency is obtained. Add the lemon juice seasoning and beetroot. Blend well.

MAYONNAISE VERTE

Ingredients
yolks of 2 eggs
olive oil
tsp tarragon vinegar
sprigs of tarragon and
    chervil

pinch of mustard powder
5 spinach leaves
handful of watercress
tsp capers
1 gherkin
salt and pepper

In a pan put the tarragon, chervil, spinach and watercress with $\frac{1}{4}$ pint water. Boil 5 minutes and sieve. Make a mayonnaise as in above recipe, replacing the lemon juice by the vinegar. Add the sieved leaves, the chopped gherkin, capers and seasoning. Blend well.

MARINADE
(marinating dressing)

Ingredients
$\frac{1}{2}$ cup olive oil
$\frac{1}{2}$ cup white wine
1 tbsp vinegar
2 cloves garlic

2 shallots
bouquet garni
2 cloves
1 carrot
salt and pepper

Wash and chop fine the carrot, garlic and shallots. Put in a pan with the white wine and vinegar and boil 2 minutes. Place in a shallow dish in which the food is to be marinated, together with the oil, *bouquet garni,* cloves and seasoning.

SAUCE MIREPOIX

Ingredients
4 oz pork
2 carrots
2 onions
bouquet garni

1 celery stalk
2 bacon rashers
1 oz olive oil
white wine
salt and pepper

Slice the pork and bacon and fry lightly in the oil. Add the chopped celery, carrots and onions, *bouquet garni* and seasoning. Add sufficient wine to cover. Bring to the boil and simmer 1½ hours. Remove *bouquet garni* and sieve.

SAUCE AUX OLIVES
(olive sauce)

Ingredients
2 rashers of streaky bacon
½ pint meat stock
1 oz flour
2 onions
1 oz butter
2 tbsp Madeira wine
bouquet garni
cupful green olives
salt and pepper

Mince finely the olives having removed the stones. Melt the butter and fry lightly the chopped onions, mushrooms and bacon rashers. Stir in the flour, add the *bouquet garni*, seasoning and half of the Madeira. Simmer 20 minutes. Remove *bouquet garni*, sieve and add the remaining Madeira and the olives. Blend well.

OUILLADE
(walnut spread)

Ingredients
1 breakfastcup shelled and
    chopped walnuts
juice of half a lemon
3 garlic cloves
olive oil
salt and pepper

Pound together the garlic and walnuts with the lemon juice. Blend in the oil until a creamy consistency. Add seasoning.

SAUCE PERSILLÉE
(parsley sauce)

Ingredients
1 breakfastcup parsley
1 tbsp chives
1 clove garlic
juice of half a lemon
1 oz flour
¼ pint milk
salt and pepper

Chop the parsley, stalks included, and over it pour ¼ pint of boiling water. Infuse for 1 hour. Melt the butter and fry the chopped garlic until yellow. Stir in the flour and add, gradually, the milk and water in which the parsley infused. Stir until it thickens. Add the chopped chives, lemon juice, parsley and seasoning, and blend well.

SAUCE PÉRIGUEUX

(truffle sauce)

Ingredients

2 rashers streaky bacon	2 tbsp Madeira wine
1 oz flour	*bouquet garni*
¼ pint meat stock	2 truffles
2 tbsp juices from a roast	salt and pepper

Melt the butter and lightly fry the chopped onions and bacon. Stir in the flour and add the stock, 1 tbsp of Madeira, seasoning, *bouquet garni* and sliced truffles. Simmer 30 minutes. Remove *bouquet garni* and add the remaining Madeira and meat juices. Simmer a further 2 minutes.

SAUCE PIQUANTE

(sharp sauce)

Ingredients

¼ pint meat stock	2 oz butter
1 shallot	1 oz flour
2 tbsp vinegar	1 tbsp chopped parsley
1 garlic clove	2 gherkins
	salt and pepper

Melt the butter, stir in the flour and add, gradually, the meat stock and vinegar. Stir until it thickens. Add the chopped shallot, garlic, parsley, gherkins and seasoning. Blend well.

SAUCE POIVRADE

Ingredients

½ pint *mirepoix* sauce	2 tbsp juices from a roast
½ tsp freshly ground black	or, if available 2 tbsp
pepper	from a marinade
	1 dsp wine vinegar

To the *mirepoix* add the meat juices, vinegar and pepper and simmer 10 minutes.

SAUCE PROVENÇALE

Ingredients

2 onions
1 garlic clove
1 oz olive oil
1 tbsp flour
¼ pint meat stock

1 tomato
6 de-stoned black olives
1 tbsp chopped basil, sprig
  of thyme, bayleaf
salt and pepper

Lightly fry the sliced onions and garlic in the oil. Add the flour, meat stock, peeled and crushed tomato, olives, thyme and bayleaf. Simmer 10 minutes. Add seasoning and chopped basil. Remove thyme and bayleaf before serving.

SAUCE RAVIGOTE

Ingredients

2 eggs
3 tbsp olive oil
1 tsp mustard powder
juice of half a
  lemon

1 tbsp each chopped
  chervil, chives and
  tarragon
2 tbsp chopped watercress
salt and pepper

Hard boil the eggs and pound the yolks with the mustard powder and lemon juice. Add the oil, as for a mayonnaise, and, lastly, the seasoning and herbs. Blend well.

SAUCE RÉMOULADE

Ingredients

1 tsp vinegar
olive oil
1 tsp mustard powder
yolk of an egg

salt and pepper
1 tsp each chopped chives
  and tarragon
1 tsp capers
1 chopped gherkin

Make a mayonnaise with the mustard, egg yolk and oil. Add the seasoning, capers and herbs and blend well.

SAUCE ROBERT

See **SAUCE CHARCUTIÈRE.**

SAUCE A LA SAUGE
(sage sauce)

Ingredients

2 shallots	½ cup finely chopped sage
2 tbsp fresh breadcrumbs	salt and pepper
1 oz butter	1 tbsp juices from a roast

Boil the shallots in a minimum of water. Mince finely and return to pan with the breadcrumbs, butter and seasoning. Simmer 5 minutes, then add the meat juices.

SAUCE SOUBISE
(onion sauce)

Ingredients

2 large onions	1 oz flour
2 oz butter	salt and pepper
	½ pint milk

Slice the onions, boil 2 minutes and drain. Return to pan with the butter and cook gently until soft. Stir in the flour and seasoning and add, gradually, the milk. Stir until it thickens.

TAPENADE
(black olive and caper spread)

Ingredients

4 oz black olives	olive oil
4 oz capers	juice of half a lemon
2 anchovy fillets	pepper

Soak the anchovy fillets in water to remove surplus salt. Then pound them with the de-stoned olives and capers. Incorporate the oil as for mayonnaise, then add the lemon juice and pepper.

SAUCE A L'ESTRAGON
(tarragon sauce)

Ingredients

2 tbsp finely chopped
  tarragon
1 oz flour

1 oz butter
¾ pint meat stock
pinch of nutmeg
salt and pepper

Over low heat melt the butter and stir in the flour. Add the stock, nutmeg and seasoning, bring to the boil and boil until reduced by half. Add the tarragon and simmer a further 2 minutes.

SAUCE TARTARE
(tartar sauce)

Ingredients

1 egg yolk
1 tsp vinegar
olive oil
2 tsp chopped chives
1 chopped gherkin

1 tsp capers
1 tsp each chopped
  tarragon and chervil
pinch of mustard powder
salt and pepper

Make a mayonnaise and to this add the herbs and seasoning.

SAUCE TOMATE (1)
(tomato sauce)

Ingredients

2 large tomatoes
2 medium-sized
  mushrooms

2 cloves garlic
1 oz olive oil
salt and pepper

Lightly fry the chopped garlic and mushrooms in the oil, being careful not to allow the garlic to brown. Add the skinned tomatoes and seasoning. Stir until well integrated.

SAUCE TOMATE (2)

Ingredients

2 large tomatoes
2 shallots
1 carrot

stick of celery
2 oz butter
1 tbsp chopped basil
salt and pepper

Prepare and chop the vegetables and put in a pan with sufficient water to cover. Simmer 40 minutes. Sieve and return to pan with seasoning, basil and butter. Heat through.

COULIS DE TOMATES

Ingredients

4 ripe tomatoes	2 shallots
1 tbsp olive oil	1 stick of celery
1 clove garlic	1 sprig basil
	1 tsp sugar

Plunge the tomatoes into boiling water and skin. Put into pan with the oil, garlic, celery, basil and sugar. Cook very slowly for 1 hour. Pass through vegetable mill.

18

SOUPS

Whereas, in France, the midday meal nearly always begins with an hors d'oeuvre, so, in the evening, soup is almost invariably served. Thus, it is not without reason that the evening meal is called *souper*. However, as in Britain, when guests are invited it is more often to 'dinner' than to 'supper', so, in France, it is also to '*dîner*'.

In the past the word *soupe* meant the slices of bread that were dipped in broth. It is recorded that when Joan of Arc entered Orleans and she was told that a banquet was being prepared, she replied that, being a good peasant, she would be content with a little wine into which she could dip five or six *soupes*.

The word *soupe* later became *potage* which, by the seventeenth century was recognized as the correct term, so that in the dictionary of Trévoux, published in 1771, one reads that the word *soupe* is French but extremely bourgeois, those who speak correctly serving *potage* and not *soupe*. In the early eighteenth century it was also considered preferable to use spoons instead of soaking up the soup with bread.

Alexandre Dumas once called France '*une nation soupière*' and she is, indeed, famous for the art of soup making. Moreover, vegetable soups are economical as well since there is such a variety of them that there are always recipes for the vegetable in season. While for people with gardens, when the lettuces start running to seed or there is a glut of some other vegetable, they can always be turned into soup.

The flavour is often enhanced by the addition of butter,

herbs and cream. Grated cheese, too, for those who like it
can be added just before serving. And one should never fear
to make use of any leftovers in the way of meat and poultry
to give added flavour.

The purées, creams and *veloutés* usually call for *croûtons*,
meaning small squares of stale bread fried in butter.

Purées are composed of vegetables with the addition of a
thickening element such as bread, rice or potatoes; then they
are sieved and butter is added on re-heating. Creams consist
of part vegetables, part *béchamel* sauce and part cream,
while the *veloutés* consist of a *roux blanc* (flour, butter and
a liquid which can be the cooking water from the vegetables) together with egg yolks and cream.

Some soups require the vegetables to be fried first in
butter. Otherwise the butter should be added just before
serving.

Cabbage soup is one of the oldest known in existence.

Potatoes, although comparatively recent, give 'body' to
soups and make a good combination, particularly popular
being potato and leek, potato and watercress, and potato
and lettuce.

Potage julienne is the prototype of vegetable soup. No
matter what the vegetable, and choosing according to the
season, as many as possible should be included.

Although onion soup has become closely associated with
the *halles* as the (now non-existent) meat markets of Paris
were called, it is also typical of the region of Berry where
onion or garlic soup is included in the wedding banquet.
While in the Périgord tomato soup is traditionally offered to
the bride and bridegroom on their wedding night.

Pistou is typical of Provence. In fact the word *piste* is
Provençal for 'basil'. To this essentially summer soup, lentils, chick peas or broad beans are added in the winter.

Aigo-boulido (or garlic soup), also typical of the Midi, is
considered an excellent pick-me-up after over-indulgence.

The habit of cold soups is gradually catching on in Britain, although it seems as logical to serve chilled soups in
summer as piping hot ones in winter. The best known of
these, *Vichyssoise*, is seldom found in French cookery books
although it was invented by an expatriate Frenchman. But

also good cold are pea, cucumber and *à la catalane*, the latter being the French version of the Spanish *gazpacho*.

It ·is important always to taste to ensure the correct seasoning. And just as cold dishes should be really cold, so should hot ones be really hot. In nothing does this apply more than when serving soup.

Where in certain recipes given below meat stock is one of the ingredients, this, if unavailable, can be replaced by a bouillon cube dissolved, for preference, in the water in which vegetables have been cooked.

AIGO-BOULIDO
(garlic soup)

Ingredients

6 garlic cloves	1 egg
sprig of thyme	4 tsp olive oil
2 bayleaves	salt and pepper
sprig of sage	4 slices stale bread

Pound the garlic and boil in 2½ pints of water for 5 minutes. Add thyme and bayleaves, remove from heat and infuse for 20 minutes. Remove herbs. Beat egg and blend it into the soup. Add salt and pepper and re-heat. Put a slice of bread on each soup plate. Sprinkle over each 1 tsp of oil and pour the soup over these.

VELOUTÉ D'ASPERGES
(asparagus soup)

Ingredients

	2 oz cream
1 lb green asparagus	yolks of 2 eggs
2 oz butter	salt and pepper
2 oz flour	*croûtons*

Prepare the asparagus and boil in 2½ pints of water until tender. Remove the tips and set aside. Pass the stalks through vegetable mill. Put butter in pan, stir in the flour and add, gradually, the cooking water and sieved asparagus. Re-heat. In a bowl mix together the cream, egg yolks and seasoning. Blend in a little of the soup and add to the pan. Serve with the *croûtons* and sprinkle the asparagus tips over each plate.

SOUPE AUVERGNATE

Ingredients

4 potatoes	**2 oz butter**
4 onions	**2 tbsp chopped chervil**
1 cup lentils	*croûtons*
sprig of thyme	**salt and pepper**

Peel the potatoes and chop small. Peel and slice the onions. Put these in a pan with $2\frac{1}{2}$ pints of water together with the lentils, thyme and seasoning. Bring to the boil and simmer 2 hours. Pass through vegetable mill having removed thyme. Return to pan with the butter and chervil and heat through. Serve with the *croûtons*.

SOUPE BERRICHONNE

The recipe for this is the same as for *soupe auvergnate*, replacing the lentils by dried white beans.

SOUPE BONNE FEMME
(leek and potato soup)

Ingredients

6 leeks	**2 oz butter**
1 lb potatoes	**$\frac{1}{2}$ cup chopped parsley**
	salt and pepper

Wash the leeks, cut small and fry them lightly in the butter until soft. Add the peeled and diced potatoes, seasoning and $2\frac{1}{2}$ pints of water. Bring to the boil and simmer 30 minutes. Sieve and return to pan with the butter and parsley. Heat through.

POTAGE CATALAN
(cold soup from the Catalan region)

Ingredients

4 ripe tomatoes	1 small sweet red pepper
2 garlic cloves	1 stick celery
4 bacon rashers	4 slices of stale bread
2 dsp vinegar	salt and pepper

Prepare all the vegetables and put in pan with the seasoning, chopped bacon and bread. Add 2½ pints water. Bring to the boil and simmer 1 hour. Pass through vegetable mill, add vinegar and refrigerate.

PURÉE DE CÉLERI-RAVE
(celeriac and potato soup)

Ingredients

1 celeriac	pinch of nutmeg
4 medium-sized potatoes	1 tbsp flour
1 tbsp chopped chervil	salt and pepper
2 oz butter	½ pint milk

Peel and chop the celeriac and put in a pan with the peeled potatoes and seasoning. Cover with 2 pints of water and simmer until tender. Melt the butter, stir in the flour and add, gradually, the milk. Add the sieved celeriac and its liquid together with the nutmeg and chervil. Heat through.

POTAGE AUX CHAMPIGNONS
(mushroom soup)

Ingredients

¼ lb mushrooms	2 oz butter
breakfastcupful fresh	1 tsp flour
breadcrumbs	yolk of an egg
	salt and pepper

Scrub and chop the mushrooms and put in pan with the breadcrumbs and seasoning. Cover with 2½ pints of water. Bring to the boil and simmer 1 hour. Pass through vegetable mill. Melt butter, stir in the flour and add, gradually, the sieved mushrooms and their liquid. Off the heat blend in the egg yolks.

CRÈME DE CHAMPIGNONS
(cream of mushroom soup)

Ingredients

¼ lb mushrooms

2 tbsp ground rice

2 pints milk

2 oz cream

salt and pepper

croûtons

Mix the ground rice with the milk and simmer until cooked, stirring to prevent sticking. Scrub the mushrooms and pass through vegetable mill. Add, together with the seasoning, to the rice and simmer 2 minutes. Blend in the cream and serve with the *croûtons*.

POTAGE AUX ENDIVES
(chicory soup)

Ingredients

2 heads chicory

4 oz butter

salt and pepper

2 pints meat stock

4 tbsp tapioca

yolks of 2 eggs

croûtons

Wash the chicory. Chop small and cook gently in the butter with the seasoning until soft. Sieve and return to pan with the meat stock and tapioca. Boil until the tapioca is cooked. Blend in the butter and egg yolks and serve with the *croûtons*.

SOUPE AUX CHOUX
(cabbage soup)

Ingredients

1 large white cabbage

2 or 3 large bones

2 bacon rashers

4 potatoes

2 carrots

2 onions

1 clove

1 turnip

salt and pepper

Prepare all the vegetables, chopping small and shredding the cabbage. Put in pan with the bones, chopped bacon rashers and seasoning. Bring to the boil and simmer 2 hours.

VELOUTÉ AU CHOUFLEUR
(cauliflower soup)

Ingredients

1 small cauliflower	yolks of 2 eggs
1½ pints meat stock	1 dsp flour
1 pint milk	2 oz butter
	salt and pepper

Wash the cauliflower, divide into florets and boil in the meat stock together with the seasoning until tender. Pass through vegetable mill, melt the butter, stir in the flour and add, gradually, the milk. Add the cauliflower and its cooking water. Beat the egg yolks with the cream and blend in. Heat through.

POTAGE AU CONCOMBRE

(cold cucumber soup)

Ingredients

1 cucumber	salt and pepper
2 pots of yoghourt	1 tbsp chopped fennel
paprika	2 pints chicken stock

Peel the cucumber and grate. Put in a bowl with the yoghourt, paprika, salt and pepper. Refrigerate for 24 hours. Add the fennel and chicken stock. Mix well and chill.

SUPPA CORSA

Ingredients

1 cup sorrel leaves	2 cups tomato *coulis* (see
1 cup dried haricot beans	page 188)
1 branch fennel	¼ lb vegetable marrow
2 bacon rashers	2 tbsp olive oil
4 leeks	1 cup macaroni
4 potatoes	salt and pepper

Prepare the vegetables. Chop the sorrel leaves, fennel, bacon rashers, leeks and marrow and fry gently in the oil for 5 minutes. Add the diced potatoes, tomato *coulis* and seasoning. Cover with 2½ pints of water, bring to the boil and simmer 1 hour. Add the macaroni during the last 10 minutes.

POTAGE CRÉCY
(carrot soup)

Ingredients

6 large carrots
½ oz rice
2 oz butter

2¼ pints meat stock
salt and pepper
croûtons

Peel and chop the carrots and put in pan with the seasoning and 1 pint of the meat stock. Bring to the boil and simmer until tender. At the same time boil the rice for 10 minutes in the remaining meat stock. Sieve the carrots and add, together with their liquid, to the rice. Add the butter and re-heat. Serve with the *croûtons*.

POTAGE AU CRESSON
(watercress soup)

Ingredients

2 bunches of watercress
8 medium-sized potatoes

2 oz cream
salt and pepper

Prepare the watercress, discarding the thick stalks. Put into a pan with the peeled potatoes, seasoning and 2½ pints of water. Bring to the boil and simmer 1½ hours. Sieve and return to pan with the cream. Heat through.

SOUPE DAUPHINOISE

Ingredients

2 onions
1 parsnip
4 potatoes
2 carrots

½ pint milk
½ cup chopped chervil
cupful vermicelli
salt and pepper
3 oz butter

Prepare the onions, parsnip, potatoes and carrots. Chop small and cook gently in the butter for 5 minutes. Add the seasoning and 1 pint of water and simmer a further 30 minutes, adding the vermicelli during the last 5 minutes. Sprinkle with the chervil on serving.

CRÈME AUX ÉPINARDS
(cream of spinach soup)

Ingredients

1 lb spinach	pinch of nutmeg
2 pints milk	1 dsp paprika
salt and pepper	2 oz butter
	yolks of 2 eggs

Wash the spinach and boil in ½ pint of water for 5 minutes. Sieve and return (with the liquid) to pan with the milk, seasoning, paprika and nutmeg. Bring to the boil, stir in the butter and, off the heat, the egg yolks. Blend well.

POTAGE DE FÈVES
(broad bean soup)

Ingredients

1 lb broad beans	2½ pints meat stock
4 oz pork fat	salt and pepper
bouquet garni	*croûtons*

Shell the beans. Put the pork fat in a pan and in it soften the beans for 5 minutes. Add the stock, *bouquet garni* and seasoning. Bring to the boil and simmer 40 minutes. Pass through vegetable mill, having removed the *bouquet garni,* and return to pan with the cream. Re-heat and serve with the *croûtons.*

POTAGE A LA COURGE
(marrow soup)

Ingredients

1 small vegetable marrow	branch of celery
1 cup green haricot beans	*bouquet garni*
2 onions	1 tbsp finely chopped
2 cloves	chervil
2 cloves garlic	salt and pepper

Peel and chop the marrow, removing all seeds. Stud the onions with the cloves and put into pan with the beans, garlic, celery, marrow, *bouquet garni* and seasoning. Cover with 2½ pints of water. Bring to the boil and simmer half an hour. Remove *bouquet garni* and pass through vegetable mill. Re-heat and sprinkle with the chervil on serving.

POTAGE GERMINY
(sorrel soup)

Ingredients
¼ lb sorrel
2 oz butter
yolks of 4 eggs
2¼ pints meat stock
  (chicken for preference)

2 oz cream
4 slices of stale bread
  baked in the oven
1 dsp finely chopped
  chervil
salt and pepper

Wash and shred the sorrel and put in pan with 1 tbsp of water over low heat until soft. Sieve and return to pan with the stock and seasoning. Bring to the boil and simmer 1 hour. Beat the egg yolks with the cream and add, together with the butter, to the soup. Sprinkle with the chervil on serving and accompany with the baked bread.

POTAGE AUX HARICOTS BLANCS
(dried bean soup)

Ingredients
3 cups haricot or kidney
  beans

3 medium-sized potatoes
2 cloves garlic
salt and pepper

Soak the beans overnight. Drain and cover with 2½ pints of water. Add cubed potatoes and garlic. Bring to the boil and simmer until tender.

PURÉE DE HARICOTS BLANCS

Ingredients
3 cups dried haricot
  beans
1 carrot
2 onions

2 cloves
bouquet garni
2 oz butter
2 cups tomato purée
salt and pepper

Soak the beans overnight. Drain and put in pan with the chopped carrot, onions, cloves, seasoning and *bouquet garni*. Add 2 pints water, bring to the boil and simmer 1 hour. Sieve, having removed *bouquet garni*. Return to pan with the butter and tomato purée. Blend well and re-heat.

POTAGE AUX FINES HERBES
(herb soup)

Ingredients

2 lettuces	*croûtons*
handful of chervil	*bouquet garni*
handful of sorrel	2 tbsp chopped chives
2 oz butter	2 cloves garlic
yolks of 2 eggs	salt and pepper

Wash and chop the lettuce and put in a pan over low heat with the butter, chervil, sorrel and chives. Soften for a few minutes. Add the garlic, *bouquet garni,* seasoning and $2\frac{1}{2}$ pints of water. Bring to the boil and simmer 30 minutes. Remove *bouquet garni* and stir in, off the heat, the egg yolks. Blend well and serve with the *croûtons.*

POTAGE JULIENNE

Ingredients

2 carrots	cupful green haricot beans
3 leeks	1 oz sugar
3 onions	2 oz butter
heart of a white cabbage	2 potatoes

Wash the vegetables, cut in very thin strips, and add to the melted butter. Cook gently for 5 minutes. Cover with 2 pints of water, bring to the boil and simmer 1 hour. Add seasoning, as required, on serving.

CRÈME DE LAITUE
(cream of lettuce soup)

Ingredients

2 large lettuces	$\frac{1}{2}$ pint milk
2 potatoes	1 celery branch
2 garlic cloves	2 oz butter
2 slices crumbled stale bread	2 oz cream
	croûtons
1 pint meat stock	salt and pepper

Wash and shred the lettuce and put in pan over low heat with the butter for 2 minutes. Dice the potatoes, celery and garlic and add, together with the seasoning, bread and stock. Bring to the boil and simmer 30 minutes. Add the milk, re-heat and stir in the butter and cream. Serve with the *croûtons.*

SOUPE DE LENTILLES

(lentil soup)

Ingredients

½ lb lentils	3 cloves
2 cloves garlic	2 oz butter
2 leeks	*croûtons*
	salt and butter

Soak lentils overnight if necessary. Drain, put in pan with 2½ pints of water, the leeks, garlic, cloves and seasoning. Bring slowly to the boil and simmer until the lentils are well cooked. Pass through vegetable mill and return to pan with the butter. Re-heat and serve with the *croûtons.*

POTAGE AUX MARRONS

(chestnut soup)

Ingredients

1 lb chestnuts	2 bacon rashers
½ pint milk	*croûtons*
salt and pepper	2 celery branches
tsp sugar	2 oz butter

Boil the chestnuts for 8 minutes and remove shells and skin. Return to pan with 2 pints fresh water, the celery, seasoning and sugar. Boil 30 minutes and pass through vegetable mill. Return to pan with the milk and butter and re-heat. Fry the bread for the *croûtons* together with the chopped bacon and serve both with the soup.

POTAGE MONFAUÇON

Ingredients

4 large leeks	2 tomatoes
3 medium-sized carrots	dsp tomato ketchup
breakfastcupful green	2 oz butter
haricot beans	salt and pepper

Wash and chop small the leeks. Scrub and grate the
carrots. Slice the beans. In the butter lightly fry the leeks
until soft, add the carrots, sliced tomatoes, beans and
seasoning. Cover with 2½ pints of water, bring to the boil
and simmer 30 minutes. Add the ketchup 5 minutes before
serving.

VELOUTÉ DE NAVETS
(turnip soup)

Ingredients
½ lb turnips
2 large potatoes
2 onions
2 oz butter

2 oz cream
breakfastcupful stale
  bread
½ cup chopped parsley
salt and pepper

Slice the onions and fry in the butter until yellow. Add
the prepared potatoes and turnips, the bread and seasoning.
Cover with 2½ pints of water, bring to the boil and simmer
1 hour. Pass through vegetable mill and return to pan with
the cream and parsley. Re-heat, blending well.

SOUPE A L'OIGNON (1)
(onion soup)

Ingredients
4 large onions
2 oz butter
2 pints meat stock

3 oz grated cheese
1 tbsp milk
salt and pepper
stale bread

Slice the onions and fry in the butter until yellow. Add
stock and seasoning, and simmer half an hour. Pour into a
deep ovenproof dish. Soften the cheese in the milk and
spread on sufficient slices of bread to cover the surface of
the soup. Bake in a hot oven until the cheese is golden.

SOUPE A L'OIGNON (2)

Ingredients
4 large onions
2 oz butter
2 pints milk

breakfastcupful vermicelli
1 dsp flour
salt and pepper

Slice the onions and fry in the butter until yellow. Stir in the flour, add half a pint of water and the seasoning, and boil 10 minutes. Add the milk and vermicelli and simmer a further 5 minutes.

SOUPE A L'OSEILLE
(sorrel soup)

See **POTAGE GERMINY.**

POTAGE PARMENTIER
(potato soup)

Ingredients
½lb floury potatoes
2 oz butter
½ pint milk

2 pints meat stock
1 tbsp chopped parsley
salt and pepper
croûtons

Peel the potatoes and boil in the meat stock with the seasoning and parsley for half an hour. Pass through vegetable mill and return to pan with the milk. Heat through and serve with the *croûtons*.

SOUPE PAYSANNE

Ingredients
½ lb carrots
2 small turnips
1 parsnip
3 leeks
2 celery stalks

2 oz butter
4 slices stale bread
salt and pepper
2½ pints meat stock
½ pint *Potage St. Germain*
  (see below)

Prepare all the vegetables, chopping finely, and put in pan with the butter over low heat for 5 minutes. Add the stock and seasoning, bring to the boil and simmer 1 hour. Add the *potage St. Germain* and heat through. Put a bread slice in each soup plate and pour the soup over these.

SOUPE PELOU
(radish soup)

Ingredients

1 bunch of radishes	2 garlic cloves
4 potatoes	*croûtons*
pinch of nutmeg	salt

Put the prepared radishes, garlic and potatoes in a pan together with the salt and nutmeg. Cover with 2½ pints of water, bring to the boil and simmer until tender. Pass through vegetable mill and serve with the *croûtons*.

SOUPE AU PISTOU
(vegetable soup from Provence)

Ingredients

cupful chopped basil	2 potatoes
2 tbsp olive oil	1 celery stalk
2 garlic cloves	2 onions
¼ lb green haricot beans	salt and pepper
2 tomatoes	2 oz grated Parmesan
3 leeks	cheese
	cupful vermicelli

Prepare all the vegetables, chopping small, and put in pan with the seasoning and 2¼ pints of water. Boil half an hour. Add vermicelli and cook a further 10 minutes. In a bowl pound together the basil and garlic and add, gradually, the oil. Add this to the soup and sprinkle with the Parmesan on serving.

POTAGE ST. GERMAIN
(green pea soup)

Ingredients

¼ lb shelled peas	2 oz butter
1 onion	3 or 4 lettuce leaves
2¼ pints meat stock	3 or 4 sorrel leaves
pinch of sugar	1 tbsp chopped chervil
	salt and pepper

Boil the peas in the stock with the onion and seasoning until tender. Sieve. Melt the butter and add the chopped lettuce and sorrel leaves and the chervil. Toss for a few minutes and add the sieved peas and their liquid together with the sugar. Heat through.

POTAGE AUX PETITS POIS FRAIS
(chilled green pea soup)

Ingredients
¼ lb shelled peas
1 potato
1 onion
heart of a lettuce
1 tsp sugar

¼ cup chopped parsley and
    mint
2¼ pints meat stock
    (preferably chicken)
juice of half a lemon
2 oz cream

Prepare the vegetables and boil the peas, lettuce, onion and potato in the stock for 30 minutes. Sieve. Stir in the sugar, seasoning, lemon juice and cream. Refrigerate and sprinkle with the parsley and mint on serving.

POTAGE AUX POIS CASSÉS
(split pea soup)

Ingredients
¼ lb split peas
slice of smoked pork or 2
    bacon rashers

3 medium-sized potatoes
salt and pepper
croûtons

Soak the peas overnight. Drain, add the potatoes, pork and seasoning, and put in a pan with the seasoning and 2½ pints of fresh water. Bring to the boil and simmer until tender. Remove pork and pass through vegetable mill. Re-heat and serve with the *croûtons*.

SOUPE AUX POIS CHICHES
(chick pea soup)

Ingredients
¼ lb chick peas
2 bacon rashers
1 small white cabbage

2 garlic cloves
2 bayleaves
2 oz olive oil
salt and pepper

Soak the peas for 24 hours. Put in a pan, cover with fresh water and a pinch of bicarbonate of soda and boil for 20 minutes. Meanwhile lightly fry the chopped bacon rashers in the oil with the garlic and shredded cabbage. Drain the peas and add together with 2½ pints of water, the seasoning and bayleaves. Bring to the boil and simmer until really tender (between 2 and 3 hours).

SOUPE AU POTIRON
(pumpkin soup)

Ingredients
2 slices of pumpkin
1 dsp of sugar
1½ pints milk

2 tbsp tapioca
2 oz butter
salt and pepper
croûtons

Prepare the pumpkin, removing seeds, and put into pan with a pint of water and the seasoning. Bring to the boil, simmer until tender and pass through vegetable mill. Return to pan, together with the cooking water, the milk, sugar and tapioca. Boil until the tapioca is cooked and serve with the *croûtons.*

SOUPE PROVENÇALE

Ingredients
4 potatoes
4 tomatoes
sprig of thyme
2 oz butter
cupful small onions

2 tbsp each chopped
  chervil and chives
salt and pepper
1 oz olive oil
slices of toast rubbed with
  garlic

Put the peeled and sliced potatoes and tomatoes in a pan together with thyme and seasoning. Bring to the boil and simmer 40 minutes. Pass through vegetable mill, having removed thyme. Heat the olive oil and lightly fry the onions until yellow. Add the sieved tomatoes and potatoes together with their liquid and the chervil. Heat through. Put a slice of garlic-rubbed toast in each soup plate and pour the soup over them.

CRÈME DE SALSIFIS
(cream of salsify soup)

Ingredients

6 medium-sized salsify
1 oz flour
½ pint milk

2 oz butter
½ cup chopped parsley
salt and pepper
croûtons

Wash well the salsify and scrape, putting, as each is ready, into water to which vinegar has been added to prevent them from losing their colour. Cut into small pieces and put in pan with seasoning and a pint of water. Bring to the boil and simmer 1 hour. Pass through vegetable mill, retaining the liquid. Melt the butter, stir in the flour and add, gradually, the milk. Stir until it thickens. Add the sieved salsify and the liquid and re-heat. Sprinkle with the parsley and serve with the *croûtons*.

SOUPE AUX TOMATES
(tomato soup)

Ingredients

4 large tomatoes
2 large onions
6 leeks

3 medium-sized potatoes
salt and pepper
2 oz butter

Chop the leeks and onions and fry lightly in the butter until yellow. Add the potatoes, tomatoes and seasoning. Cover with 2½ pints of water. Bring to the boil and simmer half an hour. Sieve and re-heat.

VELOUTÉ DE TOMATES

Ingredients

4 large tomatoes
3 potatoes
2 oz cream
2 oz butter

1 oz flour
breakfastcupful of rice
salt and Cayenne pepper
½ cup finely chopped
    chervil

Slice the potatoes and tomatoes and put in pan with the seasoning and 2½ pints of water. Bring to the boil and simmer 30 minutes. Sieve. Melt the butter, stir in the flour and add, gradually, the cooking water from the vegetables. Add the sieved tomatoes and potatoes together with the rice and cook a further 10 minutes, blending well. Sprinkle with the chervil on serving.

CRÈME DE TOPINAMBOURS
(cream of Jerusalem artichokes)

Ingredients

¼ lb artichokes	pinch of nutmeg
4 medium-sized potatoes	1 tbsp flour
1 tbsp chopped chervil	salt and pepper
2 oz butter	½ pint milk

Peel and chop the artichokes and put in pan with the peeled potatoes and seasoning. Cover with 2 pints of water and simmer until tender. Melt the butter, stir in the flour and add, gradually, the milk. Add the sieved artichokes and their liquid together with the nutmeg and chervil. Heat through.

SOUPE TOURANGELLE

Ingredients

2 oz butter	¼ lb pork or 6 bacon
2 turnips	rashers
1 parsnip	¼ lb shelled green peas
6 leeks	4 slices of stale bread
1 small white cabbage	salt and pepper

Prepare the vegetables, chopping small the turnips, parsnip and leeks, and put in pan with the pork or bacon, the seasoning and 2½ pints of water. Bring to the boil and simmer 1 hour. Add the peas and cook a further 30 minutes. Put a slice of bread in each soup plate and pour the soup over them.

VICHYSSOISE
(chilled leek and potato soup)

Ingredients

6 leeks	1 branch of celery
4 potatoes	2 oz cream
cupful green peas	2 tsp chopped chives
	salt and pepper

Wash and chop the leeks and potatoes and put in a pan with the peas, seasoning and 2½ pints of water. Bring to the boil and simmer 30 minutes. Pass through vegetable mill. Stir in the cream and chill in the refrigerator. Sprinkle with the chives on serving.

19

COMBINED VEGETABLE DISHES

Although the recipes given here have been composed by French cooks, her British counterparts can nevertheless adapt them according to her own taste, bearing in mind, of course, the vegetables available.

Even in the classic *salade niçoise* and *ratatouille* one meets different versions in different regions. The name changes too, as in the case of the Provençal *ratatouille* (or vegetable stew) which in Burgundy becomes *tatouiller,* in Bresse *tatoura* and in the Poitou *tatouillade.*

The recipe for *salade niçoise* has already been included in the chapter on salads, as have a number of other cold vegetable dishes.

When served as supper dishes added nourishment can be given by serving topped with poached eggs or accompanied by boiled rice.

In all cooking imagination plays an important rôle, and in composing vegetable ones it can be given full rein.

RATATOUILLE

Ingredients	4 tomatoes
6 large onions	1 eggplant
1 small sweet pepper	2 tbsp olive oil
1 small vegetable marrow	salt

Prepare and slice all the vegetables and fry gently in the oil with the salt until tender.

PRIMEURS A LA PARISIENNE

Ingredients
8 small new potatoes
8 small carrots

8 spring onions
2 cups peas
2 oz butter

Thoroughly wash the vegetables, scraping the potatoes and carrots and peeling the onions. Melt the butter, add a small cupful of water, and put in the vegetables, Cover and simmer until tender (about 1½ hours).

CIVET DE LÉGUMES

Ingredients
1 pint red wine
3 onions
1 lb potatoes
2 cloves garlic

¼ lb mushrooms
1 clove
seasoning
bouquet garni
2 oz butter

Fry slightly the sliced onions and mushrooms until soft, taking care that the onions do not brown. Add the sliced potatoes, garlic, clove, *bouquet garni* and seasoning. Cover with the wine. Bring to the boil and simmer 40 minutes. Remove *bouquet garni* before serving.

MACÉDOINE DE LÉGUMES NOUVEAUX

Ingredients
¼ lb green beans
½ lb garden peas
¼ lb carrots
8 spring onions
1 lettuce

yolk of an egg
juice of half a lemon
pinch of mustard powder
olive oil
seasoning

Shell the peas, slice the beans and carrots, and boil together until tender. Drain. Make a mayonnaise by breaking the egg yolk into a bowl with the mustard powder and beating. Add the oil, drop by drop, beating all the time. Add lemon juice and seasoning. Wash, shred and drain the lettuce and spread over the serving dish. Add the sliced raw onions to the cooked vegetables and mix well with the mayonnaise. Arrange over the lettuce.

PURÉE DE CIBOURE

Ingredients

1 lb potatoes
¼ lb dried haricot beans
2 garlic cloves
2 onions

cupful mixed herbs as
  available
¼ pint meat stock
salt and pepper

Soak the beans overnight. Put in pan with the peeled potatoes, the garlic, onions, herbs and seasoning. Cover with water and boil 1½ hours. Pass through vegetable mill and return to pan with the meat stock. Simmer a further 5 minutes, turning well.

PIPÉRADE

Ingredients

4 eggs
2 tbsp olive oil
3 large tomatoes
1 small red sweet pepper

2 garlic cloves
cupful fresh breadcrumbs
2 bacon rashers
salt

Remove seeds from the pepper and slice. Chop the garlic, bacon and tomatoes. Heat the oil and lightly fry the bacon, garlic and pepper. Add the tomatoes, and salt and cook a further 5 minutes. Add the breadcrumbs to absorb the surplus liquid. Break in the eggs and scramble, blending all well together.

LÉGUMES FARCIS A LA PROVENÇALE

Ingredients

1 small vegetable marrow
1 eggplant
2 shallots
¼ lb mushrooms
½ cup dried
  breadcrumbs

2 tbsp tomato *coulis* (see
  page 188)
2 tbsp olive oil
2 tbsp meat stock
salt and pepper

Peel and halve the marrow, removing seeds, and scrape out half the flesh. Halve the eggplant and scoop out the flesh. Heat the oil and lightly fry the sliced mushrooms and shallots. Add the flesh from the marrow and eggplant and the seasoning. Continue until cooked. Fill the marrow and eggplant halves with this mixture. Put the stock in an ovenproof dish, add the stuffed marrow and eggplant and sprinkle with the crumbs. Bake 20 minutes in a medium oven.

FÈVES EN COCOTTE

Ingredients
1 lb broad beans
hearts of 2 lettuces
2 bacon rashers

2 tbsp olive oil
2 shallots
pinch of nutmeg
salt and pepper

If the beans are young, no preparation is necessary, once shelled, but if advanced in the season the skins should be removed. Chop the bacon and lettuces and slice the shallots. In pan put the olive oil. bacon and shallots and fry gently until the latter are yellow. Add the beans, lettuces, seasoning, nutmeg and just sufficient water to cover. Simmer until tender.

PETITS POIS EN BOUILLABAISSE

Ingredients
2 lb garden peas
2 leeks
2 tomatoes
2 shallots
2 garlic cloves
1 branch of fennel

½ cup finely chopped
  parsley
4 eggs
4 slices of stale bread
bouquet garni
2 oz butter
salt and pepper

Shell the peas. Chop the leeks, shallots, tomatoes and garlic. Put the leeks and shallots in a pan with the butter and fry gently until yellow. Add the crushed garlic and tomatoes together with the fennel, *bouquet garni* and seasoning. Cover with 2 pints of water and bring to the boil. Add the peas and continue boiling until these are cooked. Break in the eggs and poach. Pour off surplus liquid. Put a slice of bread in each soup plate and on these put the vegetables topped by the eggs and sprinkle with the parsley.

CROUSTADES DE PURÉE DE LÉGUMES

Ingredients

8 small pastry barques	1 parsnip
4 leeks	2 oz butter
4 potatoes	2 oz cream
2 turnips	salt and pepper

Prepare the vegetables, discarding the green part of the leeks and put in pan. Cover with water and boil until tender. Sieve. Return to pan with butter and seasoning and turn for 2 minutes. Blend in cream and put into barques. Heat through in the oven.

ARTICHAUTS ET PETITS POIS MAÎTRE D'HÔTEL

Ingredients

hearts of 4 artichokes	pinch of sugar
1 lb of garden peas	juice of half a lemon
2 shallots	chicken stock
2 oz butter	¼ cup chopped parsley
	salt and pepper

Slice the artichoke hearts and put in pan with the peas, sliced shallots and sufficient stock to cover. Simmer until tender, and drain. Return to pan with the butter, lemon juice, sugar, seasoning and parsley, and turn a further 2 minutes.

LÉGUMES AU GRATIN

Ingredients

1 lb spinach	1 shallot
1 small vegetable marrow	cupful brown breadcrumbs
1 sweet pepper	2 oz olive oil
1 turnip	1 pint meat stock
¼ lb green haricot beans	salt and pepper

Peel and chop the turnip. Peel the marrow, removing seeds, and slice. Remove seeds from the pepper and slice. Heat the oil and cook gently the marrow, pepper and sliced shallots for 5 minutes. Add the turnip, beans and seasoning. Cover with the stock, bring to the boil and simmer until all the vegetables are cooked. Turn into an ovenproof dish. Sprinkle with the breadcrumbs and bake 10 minutes.

CROÛTES FORESTIÈRES

Ingredients

4 thick slices of stale bread	$\frac{1}{4}$ lb mushrooms
	2 oz olive oil
2 oz butter	pinch of nutmeg
4 bacon rashers	1 oz flour
8 shallots	$\frac{1}{2}$ pint white wine
2 large carrots	$\frac{1}{4}$ cup chopped parsley
	salt and pepper

Peel and slice the shallots, scrub and slice mushrooms. Slice the carrots and boil 10 minutes. Melt the butter and lightly fry the chopped bacon rashers, mushrooms and shallots. Add carrots, seasoning, nutmeg and flour. Blend well and add the wine. Simmer 10 minutes. During this time scoop out crumb from the bread slices and brown lightly in the oven. Fill with the bacon and vegetable mixture, top with the parsley and serve immediately.

LÉGUMES RISSOLÉS

Ingredients

1 large onion	2 oz flour
1 stalk celery	2 potatoes
2 carrots	salt and pepper
$\frac{1}{4}$ lb green haricot beans	2 oz butter
1 egg	browned breadcrumbs

Prepare the vegetables and lightly fry the sliced onion, celery and grated carrots. Add the previously boiled potatoes and beans. Remove from heat and add the seasoning, beaten egg and flour. Form into balls, flattening top and bottom, dip in a little milk, flour and the breadcrumbs and fry until golden. Serve with a tomato sauce (see page 187).

LÉGUMES A L'ALSACIENNE

Ingredients

1 cup dried haricot beans	2 cups flour
¼ lb mushrooms	1 tbsp tomato ketchup
2 onions	3 oz butter
2 tomatoes	sprigs of thyme and
	rosemary

Soak the beans overnight. Boil and drain. Melt 2 oz of the butter and lightly fry the sliced onions and mushrooms. Add the tomatoes, seasoning, thyme and rosemary. Make dumplings with the flour, a little milk and the remaining butter and put into fast boiling water until they rise to the surface. Drain and add to the vegetables. Continue cooking a further 10 minutes.

SALADE CATALANE

Ingredients

1 small cucumber	1 cup fresh breadcrumbs
1 lb tomatoes	juice of half a lemon
1 red sweet pepper	2 tbsp olive oil
2 garlic cloves	salt and pepper

Peel and chop the cucumber. Remove seeds from pepper and slice the tomatoes. Put all these in a pan together with the breadcrumbs. Add sufficient water to cover, bring to the boil and simmer 20 minutes. Sieve, add seasoning, lemon juice and oil and refrigerate.

LÉGUMES EN GELÉE

Ingredients

1 oz powdered gelatine	1 cup shelled peas
2 medium-sized carrots	1 shallot
2 tbsp tomato *coulis*	6 cauliflower florets
(see page 188)	2 small tomatoes
juice of half a lemon	salt and pepper

Scrub the carrots, cut into rounds and boil 10 minutes. Drain. Boil and drain the peas. Heat the tomato *coulis* and in it dissolve the gelatine. When on the verge of setting pour a little into a mould so that the bottom is completely covered. Arrange the carrot rounds. Mix the remainder of the gelatine with the sliced shallot, cauliflower florets, peas, sliced tomatoes and seasoning and fill up the mould with this. Refrigerate and turn out when cold.

HORS D'OEUVRE JARDINIER

Ingredients

3 carrots	2 tbsp chives
1 red sweet pepper	2 gherkins
1 turnip	2 tbsp olive oil
1 lemon	1 dsp vinegar
2 shallots	salt and pepper

Scrub, peel and grate the carrots. Part boil the turnips, drain and slice. Boil the pepper 5 minutes, having removed all seeds, drain and slice. Peel the lemon and cut into wedges. In salad bowl mix the seasoning with the vinegar and blend in the oil. Add the prepared vegetables, tossing well, sprinkle with the chives and dot with the lemon wedges.

HORS D'OEUVRE DE LÉGUMES RAVIGOTE

Ingredients

1 small cauliflower	3 potatoes
1 small cooked beetroot	1 tsp Cayenne pepper
2 onions	*sauce ravigote* (see page 185)

Divide the cauliflower into florets, removing any hard stems, and boil with the peeled potatoes and onions for half an hour. Drain. When cold mix well with the *sauce ravigote* to which the Cayenne pepper has been added.

SALADE PRINTANIÈRE

Ingredients

1 large lettuce	6 young carrots
2 celery branches	1 lb peas
1 small cucumber	salt and pepper
4 spring onions	2 tbsp olive oil
	1 dsp vinegar

Shell the peas and boil until tender. Peel and slice the cucumber, chop the celery and onions, grate the carrot and shred the lettuce. In salad bowl mix the seasoning with the vinegar and blend in the olive oil. Add the drained peas, celery, onions and lettuce and toss well.

SALADE A LA SAUCE JOUBERT

Ingredients

1 small cauliflower	yolk of an egg
1 branch fennel	juice of half a lemon
1 tbsp chopped basil	1 tbsp cream
2 tomatoes	olive oil
4 carrots	1 tbsp tomato ketchup
	pinch of mustard powder

Wash the cauliflower, discarding the hard stems and divide into florets. Grate the carrots, slice the tomatoes and chop the fennel. Make a mayonnaise with the egg yolk, mustard, oil and lemon juice. Add the cream, ketchup, seasoning and basil. Put the prepared vegetables in salad bowl and mix well with the mayonnaise.

HORS D'OEUVRE ROSE

Ingredients

2 tbsp sultanas	2 tbsp tomato purée
3 carrots	yolk of an egg
2 celery stalks	olive oil
1 eating apple	1 tsp vinegar
1 shallot	half a cup chopped parsley
1 lettuce	salt and pepper

Soak the sultanas for an hour. Drain. Peel, core and slice the apple. Slice the shallot and celery, grate the carrot and shred the lettuce. Make a mayonnaise with the egg yolk, mustard, oil and vinegar. Blend in the tomato purée and sultanas. Arrange lettuce leaves round the edge of the salad bowl. Fill the centre with the carrots, apple, shallot and celery and mix well with the mayonnaise.

INDEX